KU-350-331

BANTAM BOOKS

TORONTO ● NEW YORK ● LONDON ● SYDNEY ● AUCKLAND

TUNNEL WARFARE

by
Tom Mangold and John Penycate

THE TUNNELS OF CU CHI

A typical Viet Cong tunnel complex in Cu Chi district, reconstructed from the records of the US Army and the People's Army of Vietnam.
A single complex would run to four or five levels deep and have several entrance points.

In the event of one entrance being discovered, the system of well-concealed trapdoors between levels allowed the Viet Cong to make their escape.
With kitchens, hospitals, storerooms, dormitories, and munitions factories the tunnel networks allowed some Viet Cong to live in the tunnels for up to five years.

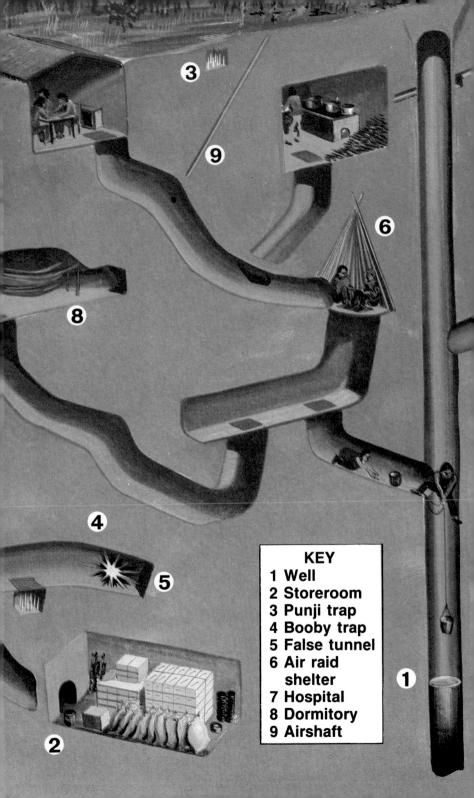

KEY
1 Well
2 Storeroom
3 Punji trap
4 Booby trap
5 False tunnel
6 Air raid shelter
7 Hospital
8 Dormitory
9 Airshaft

TUNNEL CONSTRUCTION

The Dien Bien Phu kitchen with its numerous airshafts made it possible to cook underground. The water trap (right) absorbed CS gas. Bunker roofs (below right) were constructed of bamboo and clay and remained intact against everything but a direct hit.

The Viet Cong built trapdoors on two frames with one centimeter thick wood. They were covered with rubber and filled with wax to prevent water seeping in.

HOME OF THE TUNNEL RATS

Helicopters fly in to the revetments at Lai Khe base, headquarters of the 1st Infantry Division. The Tunnel Rats of the Big Red One (the 1st's nickname) saw themselves as an elite squad, who enjoyed unusual prestige among their peers.

EDITORS: Richard Grant, Richard Ballantine. PHOTO RESEARCH: John Moore.
DRAWINGS: John Batchelor. MAPS: Peter Williams. STUDIO: Kim Williams.
PRODUCED BY: The Up & Coming Publishing Company, Bearsville, New York.

TUNNEL WARFARE
THE ILLUSTRATED HISTORY OF THE VIETNAM WAR
A Bantam Book/ October 1987

ACKNOWLEDGEMENTS
*Our grateful thanks are owed to scores of people who generously gave their
time, documents, and photographs. First and foremost are those in Vietnam
and the United States whom we interviewed, and whose names and stories
appear in the book. In addition, we wish to thank:*
*In Hanoi: Vo Dong Giang, Deputy Minister of Foreign Affairs of the
Socialist Republic of Vietnam; in Ho Chi Minh City, Colonel Nguyen
Phuong Nam of the People's Army; interpreters Tran Van Viet and Nguyen
Chinh. In Washington, DC: Bettie Sprigg of the Defense Information
Directorate at the Pentagon; Wanda Radcliffe, of the Washington National
Records Centre; the staff of the US Army Center for Military History;
Catherine Morrison, for her kindness and help. Elsewhere in the United
States: Joyce Wiesner of the US Army Records Center, and numerous
military institutions; retired generals Fred C. Weyland, Ellis W. Williamson,
William E. Depuy, Richard T. Knowles, and Harley J. Mooney. We owe a
special debt to: researchers Robert Fink in Washington and Chris Masters in
Sydney; our Vietnamese translator, Van Minh Tran; and to the loyal typist
of the manuscript, Heather Laughton.*

*Photographs for this book were provided by DAVA, MARS, Rex Features
(London), Duong Thanh Phong, AP Photos, Col. Jim Leonard, Arnold
Gutierrez, Black Star, Jack Flowers, Maj. Randy Ellis, Pedro Rejo-Ruiz, and
Maj. Denis Ayoub.*

Library of Congress Cataloging-in-Publication Data

Mangold, Tom.
Tunnel warfare.

1. Vietnamese Conflict, 1961–1975—Tunnel warfare.
I. Penycate, John. II. Title.
DS559.8.T85M36   1987   959.704'342   87-17572
ISBN 0-553-34318-1

Published simultaneously in the United States and Canada

PRINTED IN THE UNITED STATES OF AMERICA

CW   0   9   8   7   6   5   4   3   2   1

Contents

The elusive enemy

Operation Crimp

AS THE SUN rose on another cloudless day that promised only the inevitable invasion of heat by breakfast time, the US Air Force C-130 transport aircraft coughed noisily into life and lumbered awkwardly down the runway at Phuoc Vinh. It was Friday, 7 January 1966, the Vietnam War was one year old and the 1st Battalion of the 28th Infantry, part of the 3rd Brigade of the 1st US Infantry Division—the Big Red One—was being airlifted the short distance to Phu Loi in preparation for the start of the largest American operation yet in Vietnam— Operation Crimp.

President Johnson's Christmas bombing pause in the raids against North Vietnam was two weeks old. (This public gesture to lure the Communists to the negotiating table would end in failure three weeks later.) In the South, General Westmoreland's Operation Crimp was intended to teach the Communists a lesson they would never forget. With full armed might—helicopters, tanks, armored personnel carriers, and no fewer than 8,000 fighting men—he was going to solve the problem of Cu Chi, the Viet Cong stronghold close to Saigon.

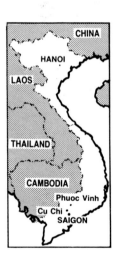

A recently declassified US Army report reveals that Crimp was to be a "massive attack . . . to strike at the very heart of the Viet Cong machine in South Vietnam at the notorious Ho Bo woods just west of the fabled Iron Triangle itself."

This no-nonsense offensive was planned to destroy the longtime Communist redoubt by finding and eliminating the politico-military headquarters of the entire Viet Cong Military Region IV, the enemy's operations center for the Saigon area. No World War II scenario could have been more apt. After playing cat-and-mouse with the ARVN troops for several

The elusive enemy

DEATH TRIBUTE:
Lt. Col. George Eyster, commander of the ''Black Lions'' Battalion of the 1st Infantry Division, lies mortally wounded on a jungle trail after being hit by a sniper during Operation Crimp, the first full-scale operation in Cu Chi district. His dying words were: ''Before I go, I'd like to talk to the guy who controls those incredible men in the tunnels.''

years, the Viet Cong had it coming to them. Now the dogs of war were about to be unleashed.

From Phu Loi, the GIs of the 1st Battalion, 28th Infantry, were to be flown by helicopter directly to Landing Zone Jack, following on the heels of the 1st Battalion of the 16th Infantry. The location was almost on top of the Ho Bo woods. Long before the sun had flattened the dawn-blue of the sky into an opaque glare, Operation Crimp had begun.

At Phu My Hung, on the banks of the Saigon River

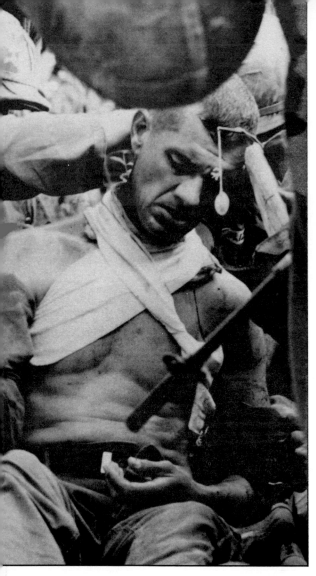

The man Eyster wanted to meet—Capt. Nguyen Thanh Linh. As commander of the Viet Cong's Cu Chi Battalion he was in charge of tunnel defense during Crimp. Linh helped perfect tunnel engineering and lived and fought in the tunnels for five years.

and within the Ho Bo woods area, Lieutenant Nguyen Thanh Linh of the Viet Cong's 7th Cu Chi Battalion sat deep inside the tunnels reading and rereading the long handwritten reports he had already drafted to his regional commander about the forthcoming American operation. Linh had command of a VC battalion of under 300 men. "We knew they were coming," he said, "it followed basic military principles. They'd bombed, shelled, taken reconnaissance photographs. All this was unusual

The elusive enemy

SMOKING OUT: A former Viet Cong, working with the 173rd Airborne Brigade, stands guard beside the entrance to a tunnel down which a smoke grenade has just been dropped. The Americans hoped to smoke the Viet Cong from their tunnel refuges: they were unaware of the trapdoor system that sealed tunnel sections.

enough to make it clear there would be a big operation."

Linh's battalion was one unit within the local Communist defense force of at most some 1,000 men. Its mission was the defense of the all-important Phu My Hung tunnel complex, one of the largest in the entire Cu Chi district.

As the 1st Battalion, 28th Infantry, settled down on the landing zone, the men could see that their colleagues from the 1st Battalion, 16th Infantry, were already in trouble and taking fire from the north corner edge of the landing zone. The battalion commander, Lieutenant Colonel Robert Haldane, could see his men were growing increasingly apprehensive, particularly when they saw their comrades from the lead battalion being hit by enemy bullets and grenades.

Captain Terry Christy, in command of B Company, knew he had to move his men off that landing zone and into the tree line quickly. He yelled at his platoon leaders and NCOs and moved all his men within minutes. But the enemy had suddenly disappeared. The mystery was, to where? A few meters inside the tree line at the edge of a rubber plantation, Christy's men stumbled across a large trench. It was the first sign of a most elaborate underground fortification.

Haldane did not have time to check the complex. He remained puzzled. How could the Viet Cong, who had been firing on the 1st Battalion, have fled undetected through the relatively open rubber trees? Haldane knew his unit was to operate here for several weeks before handing over to the newly arrived US 25th Infantry Division, and he did not want an enemy that simply melted away every time he advanced.

As the battalion moved forward with three companies, cache after cache of rice, salt, and other foodstuffs was turned up, perhaps enough to feed an enemy regiment. A large minefield was found across the wooded north end of the area, indicating the enemy had planned the area to be a permanent military complex. During the next two days of Crimp as the huge sweeps continued, soldiers began reporting foxholes, trenches, mines, and caves right across the 1st Battalion's 1,500-meter front. The men were slowly approaching the Saigon River;

The insignia of the lst Infantry Division— nicknamed the Big Red One. Soldiers of its Chemical Platoon became the first tunnel rats.
The Big Red One earned its nickname in World War I when its truck drivers painted a large red number one on the sides of their vehicles to distinguish themselves from other troops.

17

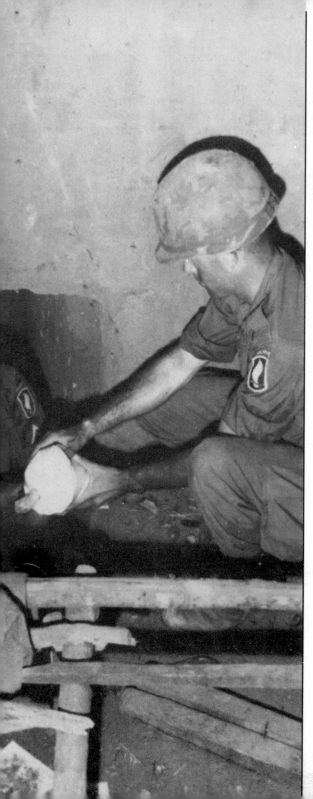

The elusive enemy

VC STORES: Soldiers from the 173rd Airborne Brigade confiscate Viet Cong supplies of rice from an underground storehouse in the Iron Triangle. During Crimp they found 75 tons of rice—most of it provided by local villagers who paid it as a tax to the Viet Cong. LEFT: A helicopter airlifts some of the 1,000 tons of rice captured in Operation Attleboro later in 1966. When rice stores could not be removed, the rice was burned.

Lt. Col. Robert Haldane —commander of the 1st Battalion, 28th Infantry. His unit was the first to discover Viet Cong tunnels during Operation Crimp.

there was ample evidence of VC base activity, but something was still wrong. Battle was simply not being joined. There were no running fights, no shouts, nobody was surrendering—yet GI after GI was being hit by Viet Cong sniper fire. Haldane watched anxiously as his men's morale began to ebb; he prayed they would soon pin the enemy against the river and extract their revenge for their own mounting losses. But when, on Monday, 10 January, his battalion finally reached the wide expanse of rice paddies that linked the dry ground to the wide, sluggish Saigon River, his soldiers had seen only two fleeting glimpses of the enemy running through the jungle.

Haldane spent half the day by the river, then late in the afternoon the communications net began to reveal that the 173rd Airborne, and the Australians to the north, had at last made contact with the Viet Cong—in tunnels. On Tuesday morning at first light, Haldane's battalion began to retrace its steps. It was beginning to dawn on the commander what had happened. He had actually walked over the enemy. He began a detailed search for tunnel entrances. But nothing was obvious to the eye. A few GIs, very reluctantly, lowered themselves into a trench and explored it, discovering an air raid shelter large enough to house several men. But no tunnels. The men, now hot, tired, and nervous at their inability to fight the kind of infantry war they had been taught to fight, waited for further instructions. Platoon Sergeant Stewart Green, a slim, wiry 130-pound NCO, haunched down to relax. Suddenly he leaped up cursing. The country was full of scorpions, huge fire-ants and snakes, and he had just been bitten on his backside, or at least assumed he had. But as he searched the dead leaves on the ground with his rifle butt, ready to crush his tormentor, he discovered the "bite" had come from a nail. A further gingerly-conducted search disclosed a small wooden trapdoor, perforated with air holes and with beveled sides that prevented it from falling into the tunnel below. The first tunnel had been found.

Stewart Green volunteered to explore the tunnel he'd uncovered with his behind. He leaped in and, with Haldane's encouragement, others joined the platoon sergeant to explore the black depths. The men penetrated a short distance and found hospital supplies which were brought up and handed to the unit's S-2 (intelligence officer), Captain Marvin Kennedy. As Kennedy was analyzing the packages in detail he suddenly heard shouts, turned, and was astonished to see the tunnel explorers shoot out of the tunnel hole like grouse ahead of the beaters. Stewart Green was last out, breathless, sweating, and covered in dirt. He told Kennedy how they had found a side passage from the main tunnel and had suddenly stumbled on some 30 Viet Cong soldiers. He could see them in the dim light of a candle one of them was holding, and which the Communists had rapidly extinguished as the GIs blundered near to them. Captain Kennedy, delighted that he had some thirty enemy trapped under his very feet, called a Vietnamese interpreter and ordered him to return to the tunnel with the unfortunate Stewart Green and order the enemy to surrender. The two men reluctantly went back down. Their mission lasted all of a few minutes and they returned embarrassed and empty-handed. Green explained to Captain Kennedy that the interpreter had actually refused to talk to the enemy. The captain quizzed the interpreter, who balefully informed the American officer that he had to "hold his breath" in the tunnel because "there was no air" and he would have "died" if he had started to talk. From a military rather than medical point of view, that last statement might have been extremely accurate. In any event, the VC escaped.

The unofficial logo for Operation Crimp. It shows the hammer and sickle of the Communist forces being crushed in the vise of the "Iron Brigade"—the 3rd Brigade of the 1st Infantry.

Sensing the overpowering reluctance on the part of his men and their ARVN interpreter to investigate the tunnels, Lieutenant Colonel Haldane decided to smoke the enemy out and ordered a lightweight petrol-powered blower to be brought to the tunnel entrance. Several red-smoke grenades were dropped into the hole and blown through the tunnel. Within a few minutes the GIs were astonished to see red smoke emerging from numerous exit points all over the ground. However, the smoke made no impact on any remaining enemy, so the battalion commander ordered CS, a nonlethal riot control gas, to be pumped through the tunnel. Once again this brought no result. Finally, Stewart Green was prevailed upon to make his third and last trip into the hole, accompanied this time by a demolitions expert. The men placed charges on each side

The insignia of the 173rd Airborne —known as the Sky Soldiers. The all-volunteer elite outfit was formed in 1964 to act as a rapid response force. Their task during Crimp was to clear Cu Chi district in advance of the establishment of a huge US base there.

of the main and secondary tunnel, and crawled quickly back to the surface. The earth exploded and with grim satisfaction Haldane moved his unit on to catch up with the 2nd Battalion.

It had been exactly two days earlier and a few miles away at Phu My Hung that Lieutenant Nguyen Thanh Linh made *his* first contact with the Americans on the sweep. He had thought his tactics through very carefully. Everything depended on the tunnels. But did the Americans know about them and had *they* planned a tactical move to counter his considerable environmental advantage?

"I had divided my men into small cell-like units. I told them under no circumstances to concentrate. I spread my men into each hamlet where we had well-hidden firing positions to hold back the Americans. Each cell had some three or four soldiers. On 8 January, Crimp was a day old. I was at Goc Chang hamlet in An Nhon Tay village (in the Ho Bo woods). The troops had been pouring in by helicopter. They didn't attack right away, they set up positions and built a command post, then their troops advanced along the village paths, two to three soldiers walking ahead, more following behind. We saw they really *were* very big men. We waited until they were very close. We were in our 'spider hole' firing positions—the Americans never saw us at all. I ordered my men to fire, one GI fell down, the others just stood around looking at him."

On 11 January 1966, the tunnels themselves claimed one of their first victims, Corporal Bob Bowtell of the 3rd Field Troop of the Royal Australian Engineers. The troop was part of the 1st Battalion Group of the Royal Australian Regiment, brought in to act as a blocking force on the northern perimeter of the Crimp operational area. The "Aussies," with their traditional bush hats and British military background, made a distinct and colorful contrast to the GIs.

Their area was covered with light scrub, rubber plantations, and secondary growth; the Australians were all volunteers and most were keen to find the action. Third Field Troop was led by a large, beefy, and popular officer, Captain Alex MacGregor.

While exploring an underground tunnel, Bob Bowtell, a typically tall but lean Australian, unwisely tried to wriggle through a tiny trapdoor

The elusive enemy

DOWN UNDER:
An Australian soldier sits guard near two tunnel entrances in a Viet Cong headquarters complex discovered during Crimp. The camouflage roof covering has been removed. The Viet Cong built this bunker with 3- to 6-inch-thick clay walls. Bamboo poles over the bunker supported a black-painted tin roof. On top of that the Viet Cong placed branches to make it undetectable from the air.

The elusive enemy

UNDERMAPPED: An American intelligence diagram issued after Operation Crimp for the benefit of US troops. The diagram, depicting a simple tunnel system in a village, gravely underestimated the nature and extent of the Viet Cong tunnel network that then extended for up to 200 kilometers.

connecting one tunnel level with another. It measured 16 inches by 11 inches, dimensions that would hardly have allowed a lithe Viet Cong guerrilla through, let alone a larger-framed Westerner. Bowtell got stuck and within seconds realized that lingering smoke from a "mighty mite" specially adapted commercial air blower had expelled most of the oxygen in the tunnel. He shouted for help. Sapper Jim Daly, his comrade, volunteered to help, but by the time Daly got to the trapdoor, Bowtell was

already unconscious. Futile attempts began above
ground to sink an airshaft to the sapper. Daly was
himself almost asphyxiated by the lingering fumes,
but he had to try to cut Bowtell free with his knife
by enlarging the tiny trapdoor frame in which the
corporal's limp body was jammed. Four times he
tried but failed to drag the corporal out until, himself
on the verge of collapse, he was ordered to stop. After
Bowtell's death, MacGregor made sure no similar
accidental deaths were ever to afflict the Australians.

Tight squeeze —an Australian soldier examines the trapdoor entrance to a Viet Cong tunnel system that proved too narrow for him. Only the lithest of men, putting their hands above their heads, could slip through these 1½-foot-wide trapdoors.

Jim Daly received a "mention in despatches" for "his sense of purpose, coolness in action and disregard for his own safety which was an inspiration to all who fought with him."

Meanwhile the Americans were learning about tunnels, too. Three days before the operation ended, they brought in a huge mechanized flamethrower to support an infantry task force to attack to the north of Ho Bo woods. The flame-thrower was driven by Sergeant First Class Bernard Justen, then operations sergeant with the Chemical Section of the 1st Infantry Division. His flamethrower was mounted on an APC, a half-track. It fired liquid napalm out of the nozzle by compressed air. The droplets were ignited by gasoline. This system was known as saturation firing—"you didn't waste any as it shot to the target that way," said Justen. The diminutive Texan was eventually to specialize in tunnel warfare, but during Crimp he admits he didn't quite know what was happening. "We knew nothing about the tunnels, and we had the wrong equipment. Everything that was learned was learned the hard way."

Justen used his flamethrower to burn away jungle and growth near trenches. If this expensive technique had exposed a tunnel entrance—some had trapdoors and some did not—then he would explore.

As Crimp and its immediate follow-up, Operation Buckskin, drew to a close the "Sky Soldiers," as the 173rd were known, remounted their noisy winged horses and flew back to base; the trucks and the APCs ground out of the hostile woods leaving burned and empty villages. Most of the local population had been evacuated by the Americans because "they had lived under VC rule for many years, consequently they were thoroughly indoctrinated by the VC and willingly supported them."

COLONEL NGUYEN VAN MINH of the Vietnamese People's Army is compiling the full military history of all the campaigns in the old Saigon-Gia Dinh districts throughout the war. A handsome, crew-cut professional soldier, his views about the Americans are almost wholly political. Nevertheless, there is some truth in his assessment of Crimp as an American failure. Nothing was lost that could not be replaced, he claimed, and such was the mobility and flexibility of the Viet Cong military structure that it could survive those short, drastic American hammer blows and still re-emerge fighting.

Operation Crimp failed to clear the target area of the enemy for very long, failed to destroy his infrastructure, and highlighted the inherent weakness of the search-and-destroy tactic that was to become standard operating procedure for the US Army. The operation's major achievement was the discovery of some parts of the enormous tunnel complex that ran underneath Cu Chi district, and to concentrate minds on how to deal with them in the future.

Ultimately, what was self-evident was that the US armed forces were not facing a bunch of Communist terrorists who had somehow infiltrated from the North and held a placid South Vietnamese peasantry at knife-point. The Americans had discovered a new enemy. He was better armed than they imagined; he was far more elusive than they imagined; he seemed to set his own conditions for combat; and he must have found willing support from the inhabitants of the Cu Chi villages to operate with the subtlety that allowed such room for maneuver. The Americans had begun to discover the real Viet Cong.

BURNING OUT:
A flamethrower mounted on an M-113 armored personnel carrier fires napalm into the jungle. This method of uncovering tunnel entrances by burning away the undergrowth was known as saturation firing. It rarely proved successful.

Digging for victory

The tunnels "manual"

How South Vietnam was divided into military regions.

CAPTAIN NGUYEN THANH LINH of the People's Army of the Socialist Republic of Vietnam spent five years in the tunnels of Cu Chi. His VC 7th Battalion was "wiped out" so many times he lost count of the number of times it was reconstructed.

For the Communist engineers, the cadres, and the peasants, the soil of Cu Chi had always contained a huge natural environmental advantage for tunneling. Owing much to its proximity to the nearby Saigon River, it is predominantly laterite clay, a ferric soil with a clay binder, allowing some air penetration. According to Engineers Corps Major (now Colonel) Gerry Sinn, who examined the tunnels in detail in Cu Chi in the autumn of 1969, the clay was not particularly affected by large changes in the amount of water that reacted to it, and was consequently a remarkably stable structure for tunneling. It was further strengthened, rather like reinforced concrete, by the roots of various trees, a natural construction system the Americans called "overbirth." "It was a super tunnelling dirt," said Gerry Sinn gloomily. Captain Linh put it even more simply. "The earth along the Saigon River is sticky and doesn't crumble. The area is 15 to 20 meters above sea level and for some six meters down we know there is no water. The water (table) was usually found at about 10 to 20 meters. We could not have expected better conditions."

Dry laterite clay has a dull reddish appearance. During the dry season in Cu Chi, the top surface along the village roads crumbles to a gritty dust, as uncomfortable and penetrating as sand. Yet the texture of the laterite clay around the tunnels was as hard as brick and seemingly impermeable.

Indeed the tunnels of Cu Chi were destined to

Digging for victory

CONSTRUCTION TEAM: Villagers in Cu Chi digging a communication trench that eventually linked into the tunnel system. Every able-bodied person in a village took part in tunnel construction. Since 1945 the Vietnamese had established tunnel networks as part of their defense systems. It led the commander of American forces in Vietnam, Gen. William Westmoreland, to describe the Viet Cong as "human moles."

become the linchpin of the entire regional campaign, and to be that they would have to survive the high-tech assault of the most powerful and sophisticated military machine in the world.

On 24 September 1976, a detachment of the Korean 28th Infantry Regiment of the 9th (South Korean) Division captured a remarkable enemy document. A full four months later it was handed over to the American Defense Intelligence Agency and all the appropriate senior command structures

in Vietnam. But by early 1968, by the time it had reached right down to unit command levels, it was almost too late in the war to be of much help. The Tet Offensive, the surprise enemy attack timed to coincide with the Vietnamese lunar new year festivities, was imminent and the fundamental nature of the land war would soon change. The document appears to be, on its own admission, the only tunnels "manual" ever issued by the Communists. It is a ten-page-long technical and political booklet,

Tunnel digger Vien Phuong —in his poetry and writings he provided a rare account of the appalling difficulties faced by those who lived in the tunnels. During the rainy season he described the soil as soft like sugar. In the dry season it was hard like rock.

revealing many intimate and secret details about the tunnels' structure and strategic purpose. The anonymous author displays the party's hopes and fears for the future of tunnel warfare in a style that mixes the authority, naivete, and patronizing attitude that generally reflected the relationship between senior regional cadres and their village equivalents.

The *primary* role of the tunnels was stressed and restressed. "They are for the strengthening of combat vitality for our villages. They also provide more safety for our political and armed units, and for the masses as well. But their sheltering purpose is only significant when they serve our soldiers in combat activities. As mere shelters, their great advantages are wasted." And, even more significantly: "There must be combat posts and equipment inside the underground tunnels for providing continuous support to our troops—*even if the enemy occupies the village.*" The document mixes political exhortation with what was to become a shrewdly accurate prediction:

If the tunnels are dug so as to exploit their effectiveness fully, the villages and hamlets will become extremely strong fortresses. The enemy may be several times superior to us in strength and modern weapons, but he will not chase us from the battlefield, because we will launch surprise attacks from within the underground tunnels . . . we can see that underground tunnels are very favourable for armed forces as limited as ours, in strength and weaponry.

The tunnels would be crucial for launching "close-in" attacks on the Americans and also provide an opportunity to seize their weapons; they would provide excellent mobility and (as the unlucky 25th Infantry Division was to discover) "we may attack the enemy right in the centre of his formations or keep on fighting from different places."

Nobody, not even the centralized Hanoi planners, could predict the course of the war in Military Region IV, the area surrounding and including Saigon, from 1965 onward. To that extent the construction of tunnels involved considerable extemporizing and engineering empiricism. The captured

Communist tunnels manual envisaged a fairly rigid infrastructure, determining precise dimensions for tunnel and trapdoor sizes. That the system grew and developed as it did—well beyond the original vision of the manual—is, perhaps, a testament to some residual sense of free enterprise among the builders. But at the outset, as the captured document reveals, it was to be simple and effective: "We must plan for the eventual impossibility of fighting from inside the underground tunnels. A secret passage must then be available from which our troops may escape and fight in the open, or reenter the underground tunnels if necessary." The passages of the tunnels themselves were not straight or "snake-like." The corners "must be made in 60-degree and 120-degree angles, that is not less than 60 but not more than 120." The communication passages were to zigzag for basic strength, but for another reason, too. It was dangerous to have straight or snake-like passages "because if the enemy detects the entrance to the underground tunnel, he will set off mines and bangalores (chain explosions) or pour chemicals, both of which are certain to have disastrous effects on our troops." In fact with hindsight the use of explosives and chemicals did not have "disastrous effects"; zigzagging, however, did make a straight line of fire inside impossible, and helped deflect explosive blasts.

The communicating passage dimensions were clearly laid down. They were to be no wider than 1.2 meters, no narrower than 0.8 meters, no higher than 1.8 meters, no lower than 0.8 meters. The minimum thickness of the roof was to be 1.5 meters —"if we wish to avoid vibration caused by the explosions of bombs and shells and the sounds of mechanised units moving above."

A clever and finely engineered trapdoor system was devised by the Communists to create entrances and exits to secret passages and from one tunnel level to another. Where the water table allowed and local conditions necessitated, tunnel complexes of up to four separate levels were built. This remarkable feat was not just a tribute to the stamina of the diggers but an extraordinary tribute to the practical application of certain physical principles that allowed people to stay alive for years deep inside the ground, and to stay alive because the very rudimentary

No standing room —a soldier crouches to enter a newly dug tunnel entrance. Communication tunnels were seldom wider than 2½ feet or more than 3 feet high.

Digging for victory

CUNNING CONSTRUCTION: A tunnel interior found by troops from the 25th Infantry Division at Cu Chi. No tunnel went more than 20 yards in a straight line. There were bends, dips, and trapdoors offering every advantage to the defenders. The standards of construction were meticulous. The tunnelers were helped by the laterite clay soil that set like concrete.

life-support measures actually worked. Air, sanitation, water supplies, and cooking facilities were sufficient to maintain a primitive but reasonably safe existence. It was crucial to the whole plan that even if the first tunnel level were discovered, the secret trapdoor that led down to the next would remain hidden from the enemy. That meant making trapdoors that were virtually invisible.

One of Captain Linh's favorite peacetime displays is to take guests into the undergrowth by the Phu My Hung tunnel complex, stand them in a circle around an area about 20 feet in diameter, and

challenge them to find the tunnel trapdoor within that area. No one has ever done it. Linh then stamps on the ground and suddenly a grinning comrade lifts the trapdoor and pops out. The point is made. A good trapdoor was indeed invisible to the naked eye. Only the most laborious, time-consuming, and dangerous probing with knife or bayonet would reveal one. The blueprint for trapdoor construction laid down by the manual is as follows:

With boards one centimeter thick and two to three centimeters wide, make two frames, one

Dangerous job —next to the point man, the radio operator was an early target in any Viet Cong ambush. Once he was eliminated the platoon was cut off and unable to summon the support of an air strike on the enemy position.

with horizontal boards and the other with vertical boards. Insert a nylon sheet between the two frames, which later will be glued together. Cover it with sponge rubber and fill all openings with wax. A single board should never be used for a frame (trapdoor) because it is not strong enough.

The trapdoor itself was usually beveled into a slight V-shape so that it could take considerable pressure from above. There was no sag. Inside the top of the trapdoor the VC then placed earth and cunningly hid small "finger wires," which allowed a soldier to lift the trapdoor inside the earth. If the trapdoor were outside, then small plants would be encouraged to grow in it, or dead foliage cunningly "planted" to make it as one with its environment.

Ventilation holes were simplicity itself. They ran obliquely from the surface to the first level, obliquely to avoid monsoon rain flooding in. Some always pointed east toward the preferred light of a new day. Others, by instruction, "must be turned toward the wind." In the deathly blackness of the tunnels, these ventilation holes were to be the only physical reminder of the existence of the real world with air and light a few feet above.

The Saigonese poet and writer Vien Phuong spent much of the war in the tunnels. He is a medium-sized man with graying hair, scrawny arms, and tired eyes behind thick-lensed glasses. In 1962 he was working with the Viet Cong in the countryside. He was fitter then, he says, smiling. Today, at 55, he is painfully thin. "Digging tunnels was our daily task; besides the tunnel where I lived, I had to have two or three spare tunnels because if the enemy came to one, or bombings destroyed the other, I still needed one to go to. So we had to dig daily. The soil of Cu Chi is a mixture of sand and earth. During the rainy season it is soft like sugar, during the dry season as hard as a rock. If I managed to dig down 30 centimeters a day in six hours it was a big achievement. It was easier to dig during the rainy season. I had a hoe as small as a saucer, and I had to kneel or sit down on the ground. I had to find hard soil at the root of a bamboo tree or where there was a termite nest. Such soil could stand the weight of a tank. We dug in teams of three, one dug the earth,

Digging for victory

LEVEL TWO:
A tunnel rat prepares to descend to the second level of a tunnel system. At first sight this tunnel system in a cave appeared to come to a dead end until a trapdoor was discovered, revealing a network of tunnels below. Many tunnel systems extended three or four levels down.

Digging for victory

DISPOSAL SITE: An Australian soldier stands guard in one of the vast swimming-pool-sized craters created by a 500-lb. bomb dropped by a B-52 during a raid in Operation Crimp. With US spotter planes constantly on the lookout for signs of freshly dug soil, the Viet Cong tunnel diggers turned the craters to advantage, shovelling earth into them from the newly created tunnel systems.

the second pulled the soil out and the third pulled it up."

And how were the thousands and thousands of tons of earth removed from the tunnels and disposed of, hidden so that the Americans would not find the telltale evidence? The Communists knew full well that the Americans had spotter planes, and sophisticated new aerial surveillance techniques that could easily "see" great mounds of freshly dug earth. High-resolution photography combined with infrared sensing techniques were sufficiently refined

in the early 1960s to pose a serious threat. The "tunnels manual" doesn't make a great fuss about earth disposal. It simply says get rid of the stuff using your common sense:

Notice: The earth removed from the underground tunnel should be made into basements for houses, furrows for potato growing or banks for communications and combat trenches. It may also be poured into streams but must never be left heaped into mounds. In short, the

Digging for victory

BUNKER SEARCH: Men from the 101st Airborne Brigade check a bunker near Khan Doung. Many tunnel systems had bunkers near the surface. A bunker was normally a chamber covered with bamboo and earth and used as offices and classrooms for training Viet Cong guerrillas.

utmost care must be taken to conceal the underground tunnel from the enemy's discovery.

And it was. Tunnelers refined earth disposal to a new science. When the American B-52 bombing raids first began, the VC simply shoveled earth into the new craters. When US ground patrols or the ARVN troops made disposal awkward, they used trained water buffalo to carry dirt away from tunnel sites. McDonald Valentine, who spent 19 months attached to South Vietnamese Ranger battalions, and was stationed at Cu Chi, was told by his Vietnamese "scout," Phuc Long, that if enemy pressure left them no option, they would actually smuggle earth out under the noses of US patrols inside the common Vietnamese crock that usually contained fish sauce. The crock was the size of a coffee jug, and beneath a layer of fish sauce, the women would have a bladder full of earth. It was as near as one could get to emptying a lake with a tablespoon.

Veteran tunnel fighter Maj. Nguyen Quot —like many of his Viet Cong comrades he was promoted through the ranks and spent a decade fighting in the Cu Chi tunnel system. He once lived five months underground without a break.

Every 20 or 30 meters they dug a water drainage hole to prevent flooding. It was 20 centimeters wide, 15 centimeters deep. But even more importantly, every few hundred feet, in strategic locations within the tunnels, the special "water traps" were dug. These stagnant stinking pits, first uncovered during Operation Crimp, served to block the corrosive and often deadly fumes from the smoke bombs and CS riot gas grenades that the Americans hurled into tunnels in an attempt to contaminate them. In effect, it meant that some of the most modern and noxious devices produced by Western chemical warfare laboratories were often to be frustrated by building the equivalent of a lavatory U-bend in the tunnels. The ordinary trapdoors linking the separate levels were also very effective blockers of gas fumes.

One of the most important secrets kept from the Americans during the entire war, according to Major Quot, who spent the best part of ten years living in Cu Chi's tunnels, was that the construction of the tunnels was such that each section could be sealed. "The Americans thought that our armed forces were confined to one tunnel and that they were able to kill everyone down there by blowing down gas or pumping down a large quantity of water. But this was not so, it was important that the enemy never understood this."

Survival below

Munitions factories and hospitals

FOR THE THOUSANDS who were to live and die in them, the tunnels had to provide the means to stay alive, sleep, eat, and—of paramount importance—maintain the fight against the enemy.

Captured VC documents carry a refrain, an exhortation to cadres to remind the people that combat had absolute priority, shelter came only second. So there were not only the sleeping chambers, air raid shelters, hospitals, and cleaning areas, but also chambers for political theater, storerooms, kitchens, conference centers, latrines, printing works, and even chambers to hide precious water buffalo—and, above all, the chambers that became workshops to produce homemade armaments with which the VC kept the fight alive until Hanoi sent down fresh supplies.

Within this dark subterranean metropolis there were primitive forges making antipersonnel mines. There were huge caches of rice. There were temporary graveyards for the battlefield dead. There were chambers where complete 105mm field artillery howitzers were kept stripped and oiled, ready for reassembly and action. Meanwhile, above, the tanks rumbled and flailed, the bombs hurtled down, the shells fell in devastating barrages. Later, the foot soldiers gingerly picked their way through the foliage, unaware that the enemy had literally gone to earth, taking his goods and chattels with him. When the Americans were around, not a whisper, nothing stirred, the earth belonged, or seemed to belong, to the dead. But once the Americans had gone, once night fell, the subterranean buzz and hum would begin.

First they'd light up the "Dien Bien Phu" kitchens. These were specially adapted smokeless devices,

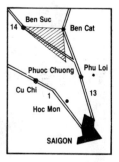

COMBAT RATIONS:
Villagers from
An Nhon Tay in
Cu Chi district
preparing
provisions for
Viet Cong
guerrillas.
Combat rations
were tins of
condensed milk
and wet rice
seasoned with
nuoc mam fish
sauce and
packed in
banana leaf so
that they
stayed fresh for
up to 24 hours.

first used in the trenches during the war against the French, and subsequently refined and adapted for the 1960s. A fire would be lit inside a stove and the smoke then would be ducted through several channels and finally allowed to escape from various and separated ground-level "chimneys." The effect was to so dilute the smoke that it was scarcely visible from the air and the relentlessly sharp-eyed Americans in their reconnaissance planes. "The system worked extremely well," said Major Quot, "but it was most unpleasant for the cooks, and there were often leaks in the ducts leading to some contamination within the tunnels."

According to a former VC guerrilla, Le Van Nong, now farming again on the banks of the Saigon River at An Nhon Tay, it was much worse than Major Quot claimed. "The tunnels were usually very hot, and we were always sweating. We took with us rice compressed into balls, hid during the day, and at night tried to cook the rice for eating the next day. If there was no time to prepare the rice, we went without food for the whole day until the next night, when we tried to come up to cook. It really wasn't possible to cook underground, the smoke was always asphyxiating, you just could not breathe, there was no air down there anyway. Sometimes we were driven to attack the Americans and make them go

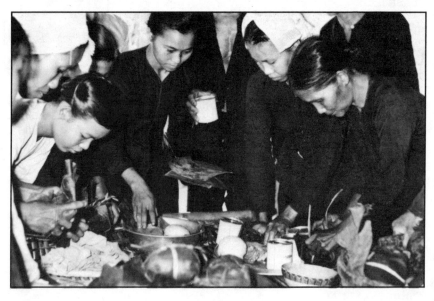

away, just so we could come up and cook at night, cook in the open. You cannot imagine what pleasure it gave us."

Next to food storage, the manufacture of ammunition and weapons held absolute priority in the tunnels. In the early days of the American presence, there were serious shortages. "We hardly received any supply of weapons from the North," said Captain Linh. "We received only mine detonators and delay fuses. We needed explosives and fortunately soon found them lying all around us on the ground."

Viet Cong veteran Le Van Nong —he only left the tunnels at night when it was safe to cook above ground.

One single battalion of the newly arrived 25th Infantry Division in Cu Chi fired, in the course of one month, no less than 180,000 shells into the Cu Chi district, averaging 4,500 daily. In one month, throughout South Vietnam, the Americans fired about a trillion bullets, 10 million mortar rounds, and 4.8 million rockets. And this was just the beginning of the war.

As Captain Linh wisely noted, a great deal of this ordnance fell on Cu Chi. And considerable numbers, as is the nature of these things, failed to explode. For once, it was the Viet Cong who began a course of OJT (on-the-job training). "We tried to understand the American science," explained Captain Linh. "We would have teams of watchers during a bombing strike, looking for the bombs which did not explode. They would try to mark the location. Then after the raid we would hurry to the spot and try to retrieve the TNT. Sometimes accidents occurred. Once eight of my men were killed when the bomb they were sawing exploded. All that remained of them was a basketful of flesh. But remember, of 1,000 shells the enemy fired at us, only 100 caused casualties, a percentage of the 900 that did not hurt, did not explode either. The Americans used their weapons to fight us and we used their weapons to fight back."

Coca-Cola cans, in an act of ironic cultural inversion, were carefully turned into hand grenades for use against the Americans by the artisans who worked by candlelight and paraffin lamp in the special tunnel workshops. First they poured used bomb fragments around the can, then TNT was poured into the middle, and finally a homemade detonator was placed on the top.

Many of these improvised munitions were

Survival below

SALVAGE TEAM: Villagers from Phu My Hung collect an unexploded bomb. It would later be sawn up and the explosives used in the manufacture of mines in an underground munitions factory. A sufficient percentage of US bombs failed to explode upon impact to make it worthwhile for the Viet Cong to maintain bomb watch teams who would emerge after air raids to recover the bombs and recycle their explosives.

manufactured and stored in the second and third tunnel levels—underground zones seldom penetrated by US soldiers.

One who did was US Special Forces Captain William Pelfrey. He was leading his unit on a routine search-and-destroy mission in the Hoc Mon area, about halfway between Cu Chi and Saigon, just north of Route 1.

It was 6 August 1967 and Pelfrey was taking part in Operation Kole Kole, an eight-month operation mounted by the 2nd Brigade of the 25th Infantry Division—a long, grinding exercise in attrition. The

32-year-old Arkansas-born farmboy enjoyed life with the Special Forces and learned his jungle craft while serving in the northern provinces of South Vietnam. He'd already been in-country since December 1966, when, perversely in his eyes, the brass had ordered him to leave Special Forces duty and rejoin an infantry unit for a while—"get back to the Army" was the way they had put it. He resisted as long as he could, and was then moved south where he joined the 1st Battalion of the 5th Mechanized Infantry with the 25th Infantry Division.

Pelfrey, who was to win the coveted Silver Star,

ARMS CACHE:
Tunnel rats from the 2nd Brigade, 25th Infantry Division retrieve Viet Cong claymore mines from a tunnel in Cu Chi district. These antipersonnel weapons were made in primitive tunnel workshops. Such weapons were often carefully wrapped in cloth to prevent corrosion in the humid atmosphere of the tunnels.

Bronze Star with "V" (for valor) device, Army Commendation Medal, and a couple of Purple Hearts during his "double" tour of 20 months in Vietnam, led his unit gingerly through the dry undergrowth. Just before 10 P.M. the previous night three GIs had been wounded by VC mortar fire. The captain's instinct warned there was something important in the area—it made him work his unit through the heat of midday, which earned him no applause. Just before 2:30 P.M. he noticed something odd about the way the bamboo was growing. It was just a little too neat. It was tall bamboo and it somehow looked a little too cultivated, almost as if it had been tied and trained for camouflage. It had.

The bamboo hid the entrance to a tunnel complex. Pelfrey ordered one of his men to blow the tunnel and the bunkers. This often led to the discovery of new access holes which themselves led to new discoveries underground. "Well, we found a complete munitions workshop underground," said Pelfrey. "They'd dug a whole bunker complex, covered each bunker with bamboo roofs, had a whole string of communication tunnels." Inside he found drill presses, little forges, a bellows system using charcoal—a complete workshop where scrap metal was melted down in a pot, and new casings made in sand-molds. The grenades had handles made out of wood, with little firing chains on them. The drill presses were ancient upright models and hand-cranked. But they all worked. The official "after-action report" on the discovery somewhat grandly called the find a "munitions factory." While it was certainly less than that, it did offer a perfect example of some of the light industry hidden inside the tunnels, which maintained supplies for the Viet Cong *and* maintained them under the noses of the Americans.

The tunnels housed the living and the dead. As it became increasingly difficult for the Communist soldiers to bury the dead above ground, the bodies often had to be taken into the tunnels for "temporary" burial. They were generally "buried" in a fetus-like position in the walls of tunnels and covered with a few inches of clay or wattle. It was offensive to leave a dead comrade unburied above ground (it helped frustrate US body counts if

HAUL INSPECTION: Stripped to the waist and covered in mud, 25th Infantry Division tunnel rats count their haul of grenades, magazines, and automatic weapons found in a VC tunnel complex.

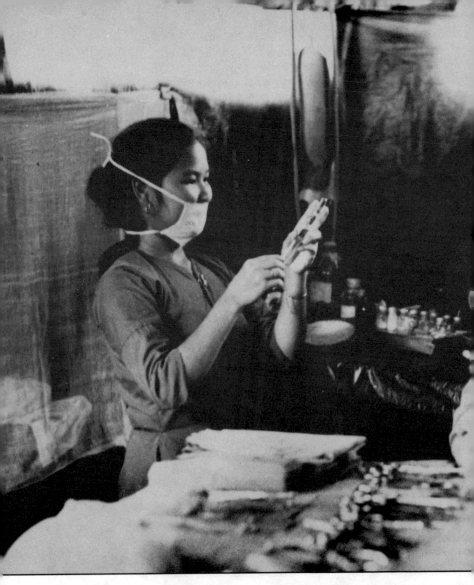

he was hidden inside the tunnels) and it also meant that the body was at least laid to rest near the ancestral home. The VC also hid the bodies of killed Americans in the tunnels to demoralize their comrades, who regarded it as an absolute priority to retrieve their dead for decent burial at home.

Writer and poet Vien Phuong, who is now chairman of the Cultural Association of Ho Chi Minh City (formerly Saigon), explained what life in the tunnels was like for him:

Survival below

UNDERGROUND HOSPITAL:
Nurses Khanh Van and Thanh Huong of the C2 military hospital unit. The doctors and nurses worked together in teams that on occasion moved location whenever a big US sweep-and-destroy operation entered their area. The mud walls are draped with parachute silk abandoned by American and ARVN troops.

"It was a dreadful existence. One lived by the hour, one was alive one hour and might be killed the next. A person could be sitting and talking to you and be dead within five minutes. With the sheer quantity of ammunition the Americans used there were times when survival was just a lottery. The tunnels were the safest thing we had, but they were not impregnable. Personally, I had a small shelter in which I slept. It was 80 centimeters by 70 centimeters and one meter high. You can imagine what

51

Tunnel surgeon Dr. Vo Hoang Le —he performed hundreds of operations inside the Cu Chi tunnels. Amputations were done without anesthetics. "Half died of shock but half lived," he recalled. Dr. Le performed brain surgery with a household drill. Since the war he has become a national hero in Vietnam.

it was like for a man in that hole, night after night. I had not dug the shelter too deep, for we learned from bitter experience that the deeper the shelter the greater the chance of being buried alive after a bombing attack, so I built a moderately strong shelter that could deal with bomb fragments. When the enemy carried out their antiguerrilla operations above, I went into my sleeping shelter, lit a candle and read books or wrote poems until the air was so foul I had to extinguish the candle and lie in the complete blackness of eternal night, listening to the tanks and guns above me. I did not know, and nor did my comrades, whether we had judged the depth of our tunnels sufficiently. One lay there, wondering if a tank would crash through the ceiling of your sleeping chamber and crush you to death, or worse, not quite to death."

Dr. Vo Hoang Le was one of the most remarkable men to emerge from the Vietnam War on the Communist side. From 1967 he was the chief of the medical section of the Viet Cong's Military Region IV, which covered Cu Chi and the Iron Triangle. He ran the makeshift hospitals in underground tunnels that treated the influx of wounded Viet Cong after the most devastating battles, and was himself a front-line surgeon, expertly improvising surgical techniques in the most hostile conditions of war and shortage. He performed brain surgery with an industrial electric drill and amputations without the use of anesthetics. He was grievously wounded in the chest, and lost half of his right hand. Today, the Colonel Doctor heads the military hospital in Ho Chi Minh City. A square-jawed, open-faced man, he talks with animation.

The sort of tunnel hospitals in which Dr. Le worked astonished the Americans whenever they discovered them. Sergeant Bill Wilson was the tunnel rat of Company B, the 2nd/28th Infantry, the Black Lions. He used to put a sweatband around his head and take a switchblade stiletto and his company commander's revolver, and go down into the earthy darkness alone. In April 1967 his battalion took part in Operation Lam Son '67 (meaning pacification), a sweep south of Phu Loi and only nine miles north of Saigon itself. At Lai Thieu they found a tunnel entrance. "I stuck my flashlight in there and saw a big room about eight feet high, piled with linen. There was a doorway the other side, and there was a long corridor, approximately 300 yards long, with beds down the side of it, with these rolled-open mattresses. It was a vast underground hospital. At the far end I could see candles burning. There were operating rooms. We found all kinds of medicine. Medicine donated by the Quakers in Pennsylvania; most of the supplies and medication were French. There were two operating rooms down there with oxygen tanks." One operating theater was, he noticed, ventilated by an ingenious air hole with a candle positioned at its base. This had the effect of sucking the hot stale air up into the shaft. Seriously wounded Viet Cong were lowered onto the operating table by a primitive elevator, a door-shaped board that was lowered 15 feet down from the surface to slide the patient onto the table. Wilson noticed canvas bags containing parts of human bodies. In all, he found eight hospital wards underground. It was one of a succession of underground hospitals that the tunnel rats discovered over the years in Vietnam.

Typically, there were two kinds of Viet Cong hospital. One was a forward aid station near the battlefield for emergency treatment, sometimes called a "dispensary." It was normally located in a tunnel complex and manned by a semiqualified physician's assistant, nurses, and aid-men. The full-scale regimental or district hospital would be back in a safer area, made up of bamboo-walled bunkers with camouflaged palm-leaf roofs, and had connecting tunnels and bomb shelters underground. There a surgeon would operate in a fully equipped theater with an assistant and an anesthetist. The aid station could accommodate about 30 patients; the hospital, 100 or more. As ever, Viet Cong medics stole their enemies' equipment, or cannibalized their enemies' products, whenever possible. The walls of their underground operating theaters were lined with parachute nylon. Surgical instruments were made with the metal from downed helicopters (tunnel rat Harold Roper once found an aero-engine in a tunnel, in the process of disassembly). The plastic tube that coated the electric wire that detonated a claymore mine was used for blood transfusions instead of polythene hoses.

Electric power was a constant problem in the tunnels, supplied at best by Honda motorcycle engines

Improvised equipment —a cooking pot that served as a sterilizing unit for medical instruments in the subterranean hospitals.

Survival below

UNDERGROUND THEATER: An entertainment troupe performing in the tunnel base at An Nhon Tay. They helped keep up the morale of the tunnel fighters, doing below ground for the Viet Cong what Bob Hope was doing above ground for US troops. The sign behind the performers translates: "Nothing is better than liberty."

used as generators, at worst by adapted bicycles. Such luxuries as X-ray machines were found only in the safest rear areas near Cambodia. For operations, surgeons wore gowns but had no rubber gloves. They wore lamps like miners' on their heads. Their instruments were sterilized in pressure cookers. Like their American counterparts, when battle raged above them, they worked to the point of exhaustion to save lives. Vo Hoang Le performed more than 80 operations over three days and nights in the aftermath of Operation Cedar Falls, snatching a few minutes' sleep between each one.

In a comment that might have been made

Tunnel performer Hong Nhung, a dancer with the Cu Chi entertainment group, performing a sketch about Saigon newspaper boys by the light of an air shaft.

specifically about the tunnel-dwellers of Cu Chi, Robert McNamara, when secretary of defense, reminding his audience of the ineffectiveness of America's bombing strategy in North Vietnam, said: "Their economy is agrarian and simple, their population unfamiliar with the modern comforts and conveniences that most of us in the Western world take for granted . . . their morale has not been broken since they are accustomed to discipline and are no strangers to deprivation and death."

Even as he was making this prescient assessment, the district of Cu Chi was already on its way to becoming the Land of Iron.

The Tunnel Rats

4

The below ground elite

TUNNELS for hospitals, for hiding, for fighting—the American commanders arriving in Vietnam had never come across anything like them before. After initial bruising experiences, it became clear that they would need to develop a new military skill in tunnel warfare, and develop it fast.

In Operation Crimp in January 1966 the US Army's commanders were astonished by the scale and extent of the Viet Cong tunnel systems. Tunnel exploration and destruction was entirely ad hoc. There was apparently no body of knowledge or experience upon which to draw. US soldiers improvised crawling and measuring techniques; some died underground by suffocation when smoke grenades had been used, others from Viet Cong booby traps and mines. A confidential report, "Operations Against Tunnel Complexes," issued by MACV (Military Assistance Command Vietnam), listed the inherent dangers of underground exploration. As well as citing bad air and booby traps, it included somewhat superfluously, "VC still in the tunnel." But its main recommendation was the creation of a specialist soldier, a new military skill unique to the Vietnam War:

NON GRATUM ANUS RODENTUM

The badge of the Tunnel Rats. The dog Latin motto translates: "Not worth a rat's ass."

A trained tunnel team is essential to the expeditious and thorough exploitation and denial of Viet Cong tunnels. Tunnel teams should be in a ready status to provide immediate expert assistance when tunnels are discovered. Tunnel team members should be volunteers. Claustrophobia and panic could well cause the failure of the team's mission or the death of its members.

The Tunnel Rats

BURNING THE AIR:
A tunnel entrance is sealed with sandbags while it is pumped full of acetylene gas manufactured in a generator. The gas was then ignited. It burned with a sudden flash and had an explosive effect on the tunnel walls.
Acetylene gas also consumed all the oxygen in the tunnels, making it impossible to breathe.
INSET: Measuring soil density to establish how much acetylene was required.

The creation of those teams would prove one of the more extraordinary phenomena in the history of American arms: the birth of an infantryman who rejoiced in the undignified but menacing title of "Tunnel Rat."

If Sergeant Stewart Green was the first reluctant tunnel explorer in Vietnam, Captain Herbert Thornton was the first of the new tunnel rats. Although the 25th Infantry Division originally called them "tunnel runners" and the Australian Army, "ferrets," tunnel rats became the accepted official term among the "Free World Armed Forces"; far from derogatory, the name was a source of pride and esprit. Thornton had been the Big Red One's Chemical Officer when it arrived in Vietnam in 1965, and which was based at Di An, just south of the Iron Triangle, east of the Saigon River.

Herbert Thornton was 40 in 1966, a round-faced, balding southerner. He is lucky to be alive. He was once crawling in a tunnel behind a soldier from the 25th Infantry who set off a booby trap mine. Thornton was blown physically out of the tunnel and into the open air above, uninjured but deafened in one ear. His companion was buried and never found.

Thornton's chemical platoon was given special responsibility for tunnel destruction, and participated in Operation Crimp in that role. The infantry

FATHER OF THE TUNNEL RATS: Capt. Herbert Thornton, (center), commander of the 1st Infantry's Chemical Platoon, which became the Tunnel Rats. During one operation he was blown out of a hole and left permanently deafened by the blast from a grenade.

decided that the chemical CS gas—along with explosives—was the best way to deny the use of the tunnels to the enemy when they were found. CS crystals lodged in tunnel walls when powder grenades were exploded. The resulting gas would painfully irritate the skin and lungs of anyone passing through. They were effective for about a week, though natural moisture would wash them away. Another tunnel-denial tactic was pumping acetylene gas into the tunnels with a Sears Roebuck orchard blower, an air compressor used at home for spraying pesticide onto trees. It was imported in large numbers into Vietnam and nicknamed the "mighty mite." The acetylene was then ignited and burned up the atmosphere in the tunnel. Otherwise demolition charges were used to blow up tunnel sections.

This task demanded not only special skills, but—it was recognized—a special type of temperament and courage. The tunnel rats were obliged to perform the most unnatural and stressful of tasks: to crawl through pitch-dark, narrow, low earthen tunnels for hundreds of yards, facing the threat of sudden death at any moment. Heavily armed Viet Cong units hid in their underground refuges for most of the daylight hours. In addition, every tunnel was sown with mines and booby traps. There were fire ants, rats (real ones), and other creatures. In damp black holes dug for the slim and slight Vietnamese, most Americans found claustrophobia panic barely controllable.

"It's amazing what human beings will do in that sort of situation," said Herbert Thornton: "It just takes a special kind of being. He's got to have an inquisitive mind, a lot of guts, and a lot of real moxie into knowing what to touch and what not to touch to stay alive. Because you could blow yourself out of there in a heartbeat if you didn't really keep your eyes open all the time. There were no bad days. They were all good days if you got through them."

Why did Thornton think tunnel specialists were needed? "At first we tried to put tunnel teams all over the division, and we had people getting zapped because they didn't have enough knowledge to go into a tunnel right." None of his chemical platoon, he claimed, was zapped in the one year (like every other GI) he spent in Vietnam on that assignment.

Gas protection —a tunnel rat, protected by a gas mask, begins to explore an underground maze of tunnels. The use of CS gas made such masks standard equipment for tunnel rats when they went down the tunnels in pursuit of the Viet Cong.

The Tunnel Rats

CHECKING OUT: Perched on the edge of a trapdoor, a tunnel rat from the 25th Infantry peers down into the second level of a tunnel at Cu Chi. Standard operating procedure was to fire three shots into a new tunnel level before going through the trapdoor. Black tunnel rats were rare, as they tended to be physically too big.

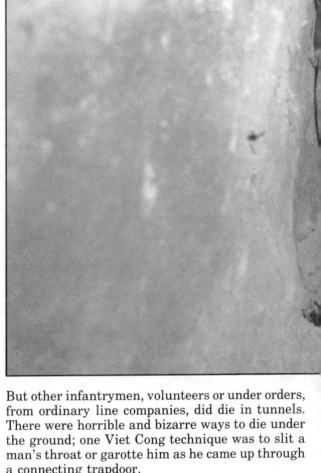

But other infantrymen, volunteers or under orders, from ordinary line companies, did die in tunnels. There were horrible and bizarre ways to die under the ground; one Viet Cong technique was to slit a man's throat or garotte him as he came up through a connecting trapdoor.

Thornton only took volunteers into his squad. If you had to order a man into a tunnel, he said, he would come straight out and say it was only 10 feet or 12 feet long when it was much longer. But even

experienced volunteers could lose their self-possession underground start panicking and screaming, scrambling back to the entrance, to be absolved of tunnel duties from then on.

Dead or wounded tunnel rats were dragged out with communication wire, ropes, or by the "fireman's crawl"—the wounded man's tied hands hooked around the neck of the crawling rescuer. No dead tunnel rat was left in a tunnel, but extricating bodies exposed other men to the same danger. Many,

The Tunnel Rats

WELL SEARCH:
A tunnel rat
being lowered
into a well in a
village.
Viet Cong
tunnel systems
often began
halfway down
the side of a
well. As the
tunnel rat was
slowly lowered
he would feel
along the walls
for the
entrance
to the tunnel
complex.
The flak jacket
may have
added to this
soldier's sense
of security, but
most tunnel
rats discarded
them as they
hindered
movement.

but not all, tunnel rats were small men, suited to the narrow entrances and constricting space: many were Hispanic—Puerto Rican or Mexican.

The efficient Viet Cong intelligence-gathering inside Di An base soon let them know of Captain Thornton's special tunnel duties; despite his junior rank, he was a marked man. Reward notices were posted by the Communists, calling for Thornton's death; there was a price on the tunnel specialist's head. He survived, however, to become the tunnel guru. In March 1966 he was assigned to instruct soldiers of the newly arrived 25th "Tropic Lightning" Division at the "tunnel school" in their base at Cu Chi.

In 1967, after Operation Cedar Falls, tunnel rat duties in the Big Red One were transferred to the 1st Engineer Battalion. The chemical detachment by then had defoliation commitments, and the engineers had demolition expertise. In the years that followed, esprit among tunnel rats increased to the point that they had a special cloth badge made and an (unofficial) sleeve insignia. The badge showed a gray rodent holding a pistol and flashlight, and had a motto in dog Latin, *Non Gratum Anus Rodentum*"—"Not worth a rat's ass."

The 1st Engineer rats worked in teams of about a dozen men under a lieutenant or NCO. One of them was a "Kit Carson scout," a former Viet Cong who had defected to the South Vietnamese government side, and who knew tunnels from firsthand experience. Junior officers of the Big Red One achieved distinction and decoration as tunnel rats. In the Tropic Lightning Division, based just across the Saigon River in Cu Chi, the policy was not to allow officers to explore tunnels. In that division, each company had a volunteer tunnel rat, usually a private. He enjoyed some prestige among his peers, but no special status.

Tunnel rats volunteered for a variety of reasons, sometimes to make up for problematic lives back home, or to prove their manhood in truly testing conditions. Once their fear was conquered, and assuming they survived, some even came to like their work. They accepted the silent enclosure of a tunnel, where the Vietnam War was unavoidably reduced to the ultimate confrontation, single combat, one-on-one; for the rats, the light at the end of the tun

Pfc. Short —almost a legend among tunnel rats. Injured after a booby trap exploded and the tunnel caved in over him, Short was rescued and taken to hospital semi-conscious. Shortly after, he discharged himself and went straight back to the tunnels.

nel was usually a VC with a candle. Colonel Thomas
Ware of the 25th remembered one of his men:
"There was one little pale-faced, pimply-skinned guy
that'd go anyplace. I remember one time he was
down there we heard a shot, we got him out and he
was wounded. I'd go and visit him in hospital and
he couldn't wait to get back. Next time I'd see him
he'd be back in the tunnel again."

Major William Pelfrey, also of the 25th Infantry,
commanded a West Virginian tunnel rat called
Private Short. "We were north of Cu Chi," Pelfrey
recalled, "and we'd run across a bunker complex. We
blew it and opened up a hole and Short went down

The Tunnel Rats

FAILED EXPERIMENT: In 1966 the Limited Warfare Laboratory issued the Tunnel Exploration Kit for testing. It did not work. The miners lamp with mouth-operated switch slipped down over the tunnel rats' eyes; the earpiece, which was part of the communication system, tended to fall out; and the pistol with the silencer and huge holster were far too unwieldy in the narrow confines of a tunnel.

to check it out. He went in about 30 or 40 feet and there's a trapdoor that led down to another level. He raised it and a booby trap went off and the tunnel caved in on him. He was buried, face down. We crawled down and tied ropes to his feet; we tried to drag him out, but couldn't. So we had to dig down from the top. He was about 12 feet down. It took us 30 minutes and was kinda frantic. When we could see his feet, they were wiggling. He was getting air because his hands were below his face. He was semiconscious when we got him out. He went to hospital, but discharged himself. The hospital thought he'd gone AWOL (Absent Without Leave),

Tunnel Rat Lt. David Sullivan —discovered a cache of gold bars underground when his platoon came across a hardboard false wall in a tunnel. After two hours hacking away they found a 2-foot-long wooden box inscribed in Chinese and filled with gold bars. Sullivan recalls that they considered keeping it, but in the end called in a helicopter to remove the gold. It was the last they heard of it.

they sent military police looking for him; in fact he came straight back to his unit. His idea of R & R (rest and recreation) was to join me on patrol. You just couldn't keep that man out of the tunnels."

They were a special breed with a special and awesome task that set them apart from the rest of the grunts. Among US servicemen in Vietnam, only helicopter pilots and LRRPs (long-range reconnaissance patrols) brushed with mortal danger so consistently or enjoyed such a reputation. The rats were professionals who did not hesitate to kill; loners who gained satisfaction from accepting a mission no other soldier would contemplate. Some were deeply aggressive men with dark and perplexing motives who found their true selves in the tunnels; others were well-balanced men who took on the job, to be so scarred by the experience as to want to suppress it from their memories.

Harold Roper was a tunnel rat with the 25th Infantry in the early Vietnam days of 1966. "I felt more fear than I've ever come close to before or since," he recalled. "The Viet Cong would take their dead after a battle and put them down in the tunnels; they didn't want us to count their dead because they knew we were big on body count. Finding them wasn't pleasant, but we'd killed them so it didn't matter. It was worse if they'd been down there for a week—it stunk! Everything rotted very quickly because of the humidity. I came across rotting bodies several times. It didn't revolt me. I was just an animal—we were all animals, we were dogs, we were snakes, we were dirt. We weren't human beings— human beings don't do the things we did. I was a killer rat with poisoned teeth. I was trained to kill and I killed. Looking back, it's unreal. Unnatural. It's almost like someone else did it. It wasn't really me, because I wouldn't even think of doing anything close to that again."

The tunnel rat was to stand proud and isolated within the ranks of the best-equipped army in the world. Not for him the standard infantryman's equipment of steel helmet, full combat dress, flak jacket, lightweight jungle boots, full webbing, water bottle, M-1 or M-16 automatic rifle, and spare ammunition bandolier. To the contrary, the tunnel rat soon discovered that lack of equipment was an advantage—the less he took into the sweaty darkness the better his chances of survival. The more they tried to arm him, the more he was to realize that neither firepower, personal armor, nor new-fangled high technology would ever give him an advantage over his invisible enemy.

After Operation Crimp, as tunnel rat volunteers began to step forward, experience soon showed that the knife, the pistol, and the flashlight were to be the basic tools for combat and survival inside the tunnels of Cu Chi. Indeed, the very reverse of high-tech weapons development took place within the tiny ranks of the tunnel rats. They had to relearn the whole business of carefully planned face-to-face combat, one-on-one as they called it, without fire support, and without weapons superiority. The rats were to become obsessive about the most minute detail of their equipment, lauding the virtues of one pistol over another, one knife edge over another. They rediscovered the satisfaction of old-fashioned unarmed combat, where individual strength, guts, and cunning counted for much more than massive air and artillery support.

Every rat carried a flashlight, and carried it in a special way to avoid being a nicely lit target. If the flashlight were dropped and the bulb smashed, then panic could easily follow, so they learned how to change a bulb in pitch darkness by touch alone, and they learned how to do it quickly, and how to do it squatting, kneeling, or lying prone.

The only weapon the tunnel rats ever agreed about was the Army's standard-issue Colt .45. No one wanted it, and very few used it. It was too big, too cumbersome, and too loud. Choosing your own pistol was a tunnel rat privilege and each sought the weapon he felt comfortable with. They disagreed about silencers. Some would not fire a pistol without because of the deafening roar of the shot, others wouldn't fire one with because the added barrel length made it too awkward for a quick-draw or for maneuverability within the tiny claustrophobic tunnel confines—indeed, sometimes they deliberately wished to advertise their presence in order to frighten the VC out of the tunnel. Not many tunnel rats actively sought and welcomed tunnel combat, surely one of the most terrifying encounters imaginable.

PFC Harold Roper simply bought a .38 Smith & Wesson from a helicopter pilot for $25 and used that,

Tunnel Rat Sgt. Arnie Gutierrez —killed his first guerrilla in a tunnel. "I'm not kidding, you could hear a man blink down there," he recalled.

M. Sgt. Robert Baer —life in the tunnels gave him a lifelong fear of rats. When he encountered a giant rat in a tunnel he recalls that ''I just flipped out. I was firing, yelling and screaming. That damn rat made a believer out of me.''

together with a shotgun, where appropriate. The large pellet scatter of the shotgun made it potentially a more accurate tunnel weapon, although not necessarily as lethal as a pistol. Master Sergeant Flo Rivera appropriated his own German Luger and managed to arrange official issue of a four-gauge riot shotgun—"real handy that four-gauge, the noise blew your eardrums out but if there was anything at all in front of you, you hit it." Staff Sergeant Gilbert Lindsey, a Japanese-American, carried his own .38, but once in the tunnel he always carried it in the left hand. "I had this thing if the guy was going to cut my hand off—if I had this struggle with Charlie and if he had a knife and he cut my hand off—I'd still have my good hand to write with, wipe my ass, you know, do something. The idea of losing my right arm was like losing my friend, I was petrified." Major Randy Ellis, who led one of the tunnel rat squads in the Big Red One, also favored an unsilenced Smith & Wesson .38, but was worried about its lack of firepower in the face of the VC's AK-47. So he acquired an M-2 carbine with a "paratrooper" stock, which folded up to about 22 inches in length. The weapon was nicknamed "The Cannon," and if Ellis led a tunnel rat squad down a hole, the number three rat always carried it. If the point man (lead man) then suspected there was a VC ahead, he would call for the cannon. Sergeant Bernard Justen rejected a specially silenced .38 with a unique light-source sniper-scope in favor of his own simple .25 Beretta.

Over at the 25th, Master Sergeant Robert Baer, an experienced tunnel rat, found that the tunnel VC simply refused to surrender even when obviously trapped away from any secret tunnel exit route. He devised one way of flushing them out into the open, by simply throwing smoke grenades or trip flares into the tunnels, which burned up all the available oxygen and sometimes led to reluctant surrender. But more often than not the VC preferred suicide to capture.

In May 1969, Baer was led to a shallow tunnel by a captured NVA nurse. There were three other NVA nurses and one Communist soldier in the hole. Baer's Kit Carson scout tried talking them out. Conversation was easy between the ground and such a small tunnel shelter. Baer's squad of eleven waited

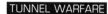

The Tunnel Rats

STANDARD GEAR:
A Sky Soldier
by the remains
of an
underground
campfire
—evidence of
recent
Viet Cong
occupation of a
tunnel.
Unlike this
soldier, tunnel
rats kept
equipment to a
minimum. The
revolver and
flashlight were
standard gear.
But few wore
helmets or
shirts in the
cramped and
sweaty
confines of the
tunnels.

out of gunshot line near the hole. For nearly half an hour the Kit Carson scout tried and failed to get the three to surrender. Finally, Baer ordered an attack with fragmentation grenades. After the final warning had been given the three in the tunnel, Baer heard one single pistol shot. They threw grenades into the hole. When it was over and the bodies were taken out, they discovered that the two women had shot their own comrade in the back and used his body in a vain attempt to protect themselves from the grenades.

But it was the knife or bayonet rather than the pistol that became the tunnel rat's best friend. A weapon as old as war itself returned to fashion in the darkness where hearing, smell, touch, and nerves determined whether you lived or whether you died. The knife was a probe or a silent killing instrument. Booby traps had to be felt for in the pitch darkness; the floor, the sides, or the roof of the tunnel delicately prodded in what became an instinctive search for tiny telltale wires, or tree roots that somehow just didn't feel right. In blackness—only as loud as the mosquitoes—that sensitized the ears close to aural perfection, the tunnel rat usually moved with infinite and grotesque slowness, each new inch holding the threat of sudden detonation, that last and terrible flash before death. There was more than just an element of perverse satisfaction, even excitement, at meeting a challenge with such grim rules and such awful codes. The isolation in those endless black holes was often welcome. Many rats refused to take communication equipment, many who took it didn't use it. What was there to say and what was there worth hearing from the ground, when every faint rustle below needed instant interpretation and reaction?

Lieutenant Jack Flowers was typically contemptuous of all the attempts made to maintain tunnel-ground links. "Nothing ever worked," he said. "We used verbal communication between us when necessary. When there was contact, the man involved would fire shots. More than three shots and we knew he was in trouble. If six were fired we knew it was real trouble because there'd be no time to reload." Sergeant Arnold Gutierrez used his communications set, but not for speech. He developed a "click-talk" by which he switched his set on, once,

Sgt. Gilbert Lindsey —emerging from a tunnel the Japanese-American tunnel rat had difficulty convincing his own men that he was a US soldier.

twice, or however many times in accordance with a prearranged code by which very basic information was transmitted to the ground. Sometimes he blew or gently whistled into his set, but he abhorred speech and allowed no two-way communication.

But the lack of communications did create a new hazard. Capless, covered in earth and sweat, usually shirtless, small, and sometimes Hispanic or Oriental-looking, the tunnel rat who suddenly popped out of an as yet unmapped tunnel hole could find himself quickly targeted by his own side!

Sergeant Gilbert Lindsey was a classic example. "I kept telling the squad who waited up on the ground, 'Look, when I come up my hair's gonna be all dirty, I'm gonna be looking like Charlie,' and they said, 'Don't worry, Larry, we'll be up there waiting for you.' Well, once while I'm down there digging up stuff, the whole bit, it's chow time for them. So what did they do? They leave the fuckin' hole, sit down and eat their C-rations. So along come brand new people from another unit, I start coming up and I shout 'Okay, I'm coming up,' no big deal. Okay. All of a sudden I come up, and pop my head out and I look around and I see nothing but M-16s pointing at my skull and a lot of unfriendly faces looking down the M-16s. And all of a sudden your heart's beating, and you have to smile and shout, 'Hey, I'm like you, I'm American.' And they still ain't smiling, and I tell them, who won the World Series in 1962 and who was the President of the USA, and all that shit. And then they start

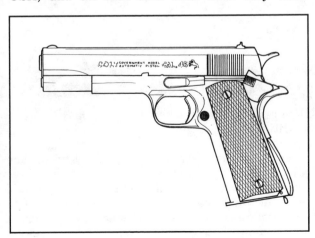

STANDARD-ISSUE: The only weapon the tunnel rats ever agreed about was the standard-issue Colt .45. They complained that the pistol was too loud and too large to take a silencer. One shot inside the narrow tunnels produced a deafening roar that made it impossible to hear enemy movement.

73

laughing, and I ain't laughing any more."

Ultimately, the tunnel rat's best piece of equipment was a body tuned to near perfection, where every part was guaranteed. The successful rat had to volunteer to go down and stay down and take risks that were unmatched by anything he would ever meet above ground. Even if he were small by American standards, he had to negotiate bends in the communications tunnels that would only just let

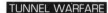
The Tunnel Rats

SAFE EXIT:
A tunnel rat emerges from a tunnel search after being safely identified by his own men. American troops, guarding tunnel entrances, were apt to assume that muddy figures emerging from the bowels of the earth were hostile, and shoot them. Some tunnel rats made a habit of whistling ''Dixie'' as they made their way back to the surface.

a slim Vietnamese through. He had to conquer an instinctive tendency to hyperventilate and remember that victory could only be achieved once he had come to terms with his own fear. His fingertips and ears became like a walking stick to a blind man. After a while, he could "smell" the enemy ahead, not just through odor but sensing him like a bat, that other creature of darkness which employs primitive sonar to avoid or detect at night.

Booby trap defenses

5

Mobile minefields

BY 1966, Vietnam had been at war with various enemies for nearly a quarter of a century. The Japanese had been followed by the French, and now the United States with its unimaginable power and fury had arrived.

In and around their 200 kilometers of tunnels, the Vietnamese were less well-endowed with money or military hardware. But they did have special killer bees, bows and arrows, and sharp sticks smeared with human excrement.

The Cu Chi tunnels' defense system was evolutionary, owing its effectiveness to a mixture of tenacity, flexibility, and cunning. Its technology often reached back to the European medieval wars.

Conventional defense for the tunnels was out of the question. The VC had neither the men nor the weaponry, nor was it ever the policy of the Communists in South Vietnam to face the Americans in large, fixed-location, set-piece battles. Anyway, tunnel searching kept lots of GIs busy, a large investment with meager returns. Primary defense requirements were, as the Communist tunnel manual had stressed, camouflage and the maintenance of silence about precise tunnel location. Deaf and dumb villagers, the VC's own "Omerta," were the first line of defense.

Nevertheless, the tunnels did need a defense system, they could not be left unprotected at the mercy of every GI foot patrol that stumbled upon a tunnel entrance or telltale ventilation shaft. The slow development of a tunnel defense strategy eventually owed much to Lieutenant Linh's careful observations of the Americans during Operation Crimp.

"They marvelled at everything they saw," he said,

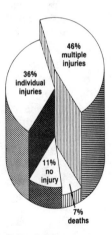

46% multiple injuries

36% individual injuries

11% no injury

7% deaths

Breakdown of casualty statistics for the 230 booby traps detonated by soldiers of the 9th Infantry Division in April 1969.

Booby trap defenses

HIGH RISK: Instant death faced these Viet Cong guerrillas who emerged after American air raids to salvage dud bombs in order to extract the explosives. Despite the smiles, one mistake could blow them to pieces; scores of Viet Cong died like this. The water from the kettle is to cool the friction from the saw as it gently breaks open the bomb casing.

"everything seemed strange and new to them—the jungle, the fruits, the water buffalo, even the chickens. Again and again they would stop and stare, even pick things up. Not only were they easy targets for our snipers, but I realised the best way to kill them was with more booby traps. After Crimp we made more and more of them. I was sure they would work well for us."

Despite the original shortage of explosive materials (soon remedied as the 25th Infantry began shelling Cu Chi), the home booby trap business began to boom. For those with access to explosive

powder, detonators, and a crude tunnel workshop, there was first and foremost the DH-5 or DH-10 mine. These were modelled on the successful American claymore mine, and were to be used primarily against the American light armored tracks and half-tracks and, inevitably, against unwary infantrymen. They were either pressure detonated or—and this was original—they could be command (remote) detonated.

Major General Ellis W. Williamson, who commanded the 173rd Airborne Brigade, recalled vividly how he first got to hear about them. "We'd been

Booby trap defenses

REMOTE DEVICE: A section of a US cluster bomb that failed to detonate is concealed in a shallow trap to be used as a remote-controlled mine in the path of US tanks and infantry. The camouflage cloak on the guerrilla (right) was taken from a discarded American parachute. Dud US explosives, repaired and reactivated, were a regular feature of the Viet Cong's arsenal.

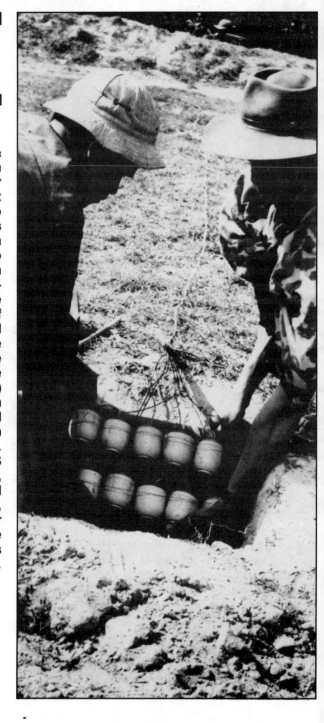

in-country only a few days when this young and overly excited lieutenant came up to me and says, 'These mobile minefields are running us crazy.' He'd lost a lot of his men and he didn't know how to fight back. And I said, 'mobile mines, what are you talking about?' We'd studied all about mines, but nothing about mobile minefields existed in the literature. Now suddenly this lieutenant, right in the middle of battle, tells me the minefields are moving. A concept none of us had ever dreamed of. And he was right, absolutely right."

Conventional "static" or earth-sown minefields had been expected in Vietnam. What the general discovered was not just an isolated command or remote controlled mine, but a procedure by which not only could the Viet Cong detonate their mines electrically from a command center, but, if the enemy chose not to go sufficiently near the mines, then the mines could be physically transported somewhere else. The concept of the moving minefield was another example of the optimum use of limited resources. A single minefield went a long way under these circumstances.

The DH-5s and -10s were made out of crude steel, shaped like a saucer, and contained 5 or 10 pounds of high explosive. The mines stood on bipods pointing directionally, or they would just lie buried a few inches underground. They inflicted dreadful injuries.

One of the most feared variants of the DH-10 was the notorious "Bouncing Betty," conical in shape with three prongs jutting out of the soil. When a foot struck a prong, a small charge was detonated that shot the mine into the air about 3 feet, where it exploded, showering shrapnel at groin level. It was a terrible mine.

Booby traps and ambushes took a disproportionately high toll among infantrymen and remained a source of great anxiety to military tacticians in Vietnam. Throughout the war, booby traps were responsible for 11 percent of all American deaths, and 17 percent of all wounds. The mortality rate was only kept down by the superb American helicopter medical evacuation system.

Real damage was often caused by the high rate of wound infection caused by the excessive amount of dirt that entered wounds. Major General Spurgeon

A soldier examines the tip of a spike that penetrated the sole of his boot after stepping on a punji trap. The trap was a shallow pit covered with straw. In the base were a series of bamboo canes sharpened into stakes. Some were covered with animal excrement to increase the risk of infection. Later-issue jungle boots included a steel plate in the sole to reduce the risk of injury.

What they lacked in technological sophistication Viet Cong booby traps made up in cunning. The trip wire operated spiked mudball (above) and the punji trap (below), with its sharpened bamboo stake, were traditional, almost medieval animal traps that still proved lethal to American troops.

Neel, former Deputy Surgeon-General to the US Department of the Army, explained, "Massive contamination challenged the surgeon to choose between radical excision of potentially salvageable tissue and a more conservative approach which might leave a source of infection." The vicious tunnel booby traps, inside and just outside the holes, generated sufficient fear among the ordinary grunts to affect their military effectiveness seriously. A high-tech infantry that usually fought only by day and was helicoptered out by night was not necessarily going to go out of its way to discover long tunnel complexes. Everyone knew about the booby traps . . . and what the grunt eye did not see on patrol, no officer's heart was going to grieve about.

In a revealing study conducted by Lieutenant-General Julian J. Ewell, former commander of the II Field Force in Vietnam, it was shown that at least half the booby traps found by the 9th Division GIs had been found by "detonation." In other words, the men had set them off. Forty-six percent of the casualties arising were "multiple," caused by the bunching of the troops who just did not know any better. By 1969, booby traps were the single most important casualty source in the 9th Division. When the 25th Infantry Division arrived at Cu Chi and discovered how serious a problem the tunnel booby trap defenses were, it created a special school, called the Tunnels, Mines, & Booby-Traps School. It was run inside the perimeter using actual VC tunnels that had been dug under the division HQ. At a more senior level, the 25th commanders decided to conduct elaborate booby trap statistical analyses, a sort of sophisticated market research program, by which data was fed into their brand new military computer—"thus giving them the capability to present and study the problem with minimum clerical effort," noted the generals.

If the tunnels' outer defenses failed to deter, the next line of defense was the so-called "spider hole," the shallow fighting pits that protected the tunnel entrances and, by their three-cornered construction, each other as well. Spider-holes were superbly camouflaged pits, dug to shoulder depth and linked by short communication tunnels to the main tunnel. One, sometimes two, Viet Cong snipers stood, perfectly protected, and shot at intruders unless and until it became too dangerous to stay, when they scuttled back through the communication tunnel into the main tunnel complex. No amount of sophisticated detection or weapons could easily or mechanically find, fix, and destroy the ubiquitous spider-hole sniper. He could be (and frequently was) mortared, shelled by artillery, napalmed, or besieged by tank. But the longer he fought, the more he fulfilled his primary function, which was to engage large numbers of the enemy, keep them busy, and hopefully distract them from the real prize—the tunnel complex over which he kept his lonely vigil.

The tunnels were not impregnable, but their strength, devised from sound engineering principles and a clever and exploitative defense system, gave them a military longevity far greater than they actually deserved. For a full five years they allowed the Communists to exercise effective control over the district of Cu Chi. The Americans and their ARVN colleagues only held a short lease above ground. The freehold belonged deep in the permanence of the earth.

SPIDER HOLE:
The bamboo cover over a spider hole. Where tunnel systems emerged at the surface, the Viet Cong built spider holes for snipers. Shallow and well-concealed, they were the first line of defense. While snipers held off the enemy, the rest of the occupants gained time to escape.

Camped on a volcano

6

Attacks on Cu Chi base

HUYNH VAN CO couldn't believe his luck. An enterprising 29-year-old Viet Cong guerrilla, he and the two members of his cell had decided to hide in a tunnel for a week with a little store of rice. It was no ordinary tunnel. The American 25th Infantry Division had, early in 1966, pitched its tents right on top of an existing network of Viet Cong tunnels in the heart of Cu Chi district.

Each night, Co and his comrades stealthily emerged from their trapdoor and created havoc with directional claymore mines and grenades, killing and wounding GIs in their tents, who had no idea where the attack originated. Mortar shells lobbed in from outside the perimeter by other Viet Cong added to the confusion, and helped disguise Huynh Van Co's infiltration. Co and his men made a point of stealing food from the Americans each night before returning to the tunnel in the darkness, and hiding and sleeping for the day. This went on for seven nights until the three-man Viet Cong cell withdrew back through the tunnel, which rejoined the larger system known as the belt near the village of Trung Lap. Neither they nor their tunnel were ever detected.

The 25th Infantry Division's sprawling base camp was like a temporary city—a military creation unique to the Vietnam War. Cu Chi base lay 25 miles northwest of Saigon facing the Saigon River, across which was the so-called Iron Triangle. It was, in fact, in the heart of the most tunnel-riddled countryside in Vietnam, scene of the most destructive operations of the war. The tunnel network plagued the Americans from the moment of their arrival to the time they left.

The siting of Cu Chi base over existing tunnels

Camped on a volcano

BASE CAMP:
Cu Chi base camp in 1966, the divisional headquarters of the 25th "Tropic Lightning" Infantry Division from Hawaii. They built the fortress above the tunnels and were soon attacked from within. There were air-conditioned offices, ice-machine plants, golf courses, and swimming pools. But nothing stopped the Viet Cong spy network from operating inside.

was, to say the least, fortunate for the Viet Cong. The American 173rd Airborne Brigade had operated in the Cu Chi area since January 1966, and its job was to facilitate the arrival of larger units. Its commander, Brigadier General Ellis W. Williamson, observed the arrival of the 25th Infantry Division with amusement. "They brought quite a lot of little shelters," he said, "little huts and things, with them from Hawaii. They started putting these things up and we were very envious of them. We were also

somewhat critical of them. We couldn't understand why in God's green earth they couldn't sit down and make themselves secure where they were. The 25th Division came in, set up in Cu Chi, and was constantly feuding and fussing with the enemy around its own headquarters. We literally laughed at them. We thought: What kind of an outfit is it that can't even secure its own headquarters? And it began to come to light that the tunnel system was in fact a reality.

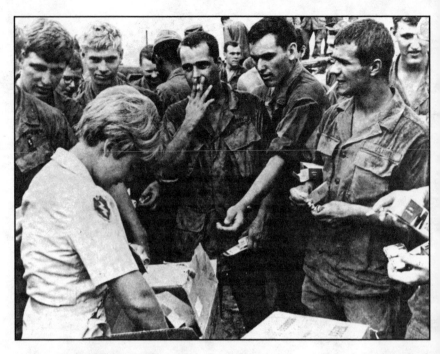

"The 25th Division didn't realize that they had bivouac'd on a volcano. There they were, right on top of a very explosive situation. They just couldn't imagine how it could be that they put out patrols— had men walk and walk over an area absolutely devoid of an enemy, and then that night—*brap! brap! brap!* The quartermaster tent gets shot up. The ordnance tent gets shot up. A support unit gets itself all bunged up. And everybody says: 'Where did they come from? My perimeter is secure. Nobody penetrated my perimeter last night. I know they didn't.' But there they are. Come under the ground and climbed up."

The commanding general of the 25th Division, Major General Fred Weyand, sent for the newly formed tunnel rat section of the 1st Infantry Division to help seek out Cu Chi base's underworld. Sergeant Bernard Justen used a napalm flame-thrower to burn up some of the tunnels they found. In his words, "Ain't nobody going to argue with a flame-thrower." He sent one of the rats to explore a tunnel and the man came to the surface—to the astonishment of all concerned—in the middle of the 25th Division's motor pool. Justen added that the

GIs got little sleep in the early days of the base; the nightly attacks went on.

Before long, construction crews with bulldozers and concrete began turning Cu Chi base into a more permanent structure. But the tunnels were still there. Colonel Thomas A. Ware was a battalion commander with the 25th Infantry. He recalled: "When the division built that camp they were uncovering tunnels for months, if not a year. One of my best lieutenants was killed there. His platoon had seen this VC fire a rocket-propelled grenade and pop down into his tunnel. They were right behind him, and this lieutenant went down there and tried to get the trapdoor up. They shot him, killed him with an AK-47 through the trapdoor. They just fired up. You had to be pretty cautious about trying to get too brave and show too much initiative there." At length the 25th succeeded in stopping up all the tunnels, if only with bulldozers leveling the site for buildings. All, that is, except those Viet Cong tunnels that would be used for training future tunnel rats. The problem of access to the base from underneath was licked, but its troubles were far from over. There were to be more attacks from both

TRAINING TUNNEL: At Cu Chi base a visiting British delegation views the section of a Viet Cong tunnel that was preserved intact inside the base to train future tunnel rats.

inside and outside the perimeter in the years that followed.

When it was completed in mid-1966, Cu Chi base was an imposing place. It covered 1,500 acres and its perimeter was 6 miles around. At any time, over 4,500 men and a few women lived, worked, and played inside it—not counting the army of Vietnamese workers who performed all the most basic tasks. Outside the main gate was a sign that read *Aloha. 25th U.S. Inf. Div. Hawaii's Own.* Artillery fire boomed constantly from the big guns inside the perimeter, "harassing and interdicting" any activity in the free strike zones within a huge radius of the base. The air throbbed with the clatter of arriving or departing helicopters.

As the 25th Infantry established themselves in Vietnam, they realized the need to give their constantly rotating troops special training in local conditions, and even to share some of their hard-learned knowledge of Viet Cong tactics with ARVN local forces. At Cu Chi base they were proud to show visitors the Tropic Lightning Academy, a controlled and encapsulated little version of the war. It included the Tunnels, Mines, and Booby Traps School. In an area of heavy vegetation on the western side of the base, 500 feet of Viet Cong tunnels were maintained by local Vietnamese—but this time for the Americans, and for a payment of 80 piastres (less than a dollar) a day. Prospective tunnel rats were given supervised and safe experience of underground claustrophobia, complete with false walls, seeming dead ends, and harmless booby traps.

When Lieutenant Colonel James Bushong was the 25th's divisional chemical officer, he was responsible for training tunnel rats. "The main thing about the tunnel rat school," he said, "was that guys who were sent there, who did not have that little bit of craziness, or whatever it took to survive and do well on that assignment, were weeded out early enough."

Sergeant Arnold Gutierrez was also an instructor at the tunnel rat school. He said that few of the students had the stability for the job, and most crawled back out of the training tunnel as soon as they went in; they would not go back and, in Gutierrez's words, "flunked." Out of 50 students over five months, he remembered only five graduating as tunnel rats.

Lt. Col. James Bushong —the 25th's training officer. Tunnel rats, he recalled, had to have that "little bit of craziness." Those who did not were soon weeded out.

Alsatian or German Shepherd dogs were schooled in the 25th's private tunnel system, as part of the dog-training school at Cu Chi. Hitherto, the US Army had used dogs only as watchdogs or to sniff out drugs in its own barracks. In Vietnam they became scout dogs, or combat trackers, and they and their handlers were much in demand to give early warning of the ever-likely Viet Cong ambushes. At the school, the dogs were trained to respond to ultrasonic whistles inaudible to men, and to detect Viet Cong by scent. This was made easier when defoliants and other chemicals had been sprayed on VC-controlled areas like the Iron Triangle; the dogs could recognize anyone who had been in such an area. However, the Viet Cong found an ingenious way to foil the dogs. Having acquired quantities of American toilet soap on the black market, or stolen it from base camps, they made a practice of washing with it, thus giving off a scent immediately recognizable to the dogs as friendly. Pepper spread

on the ground distracted bloodhounds from tunnel entrances.

Dogs proved to be of little use in tunnel exploration. The main reason was their inability to spot booby traps. In tunnels, dogs were often killed or maimed by wire-triggered grenades; this was so distressing to the handlers that they refused to send dogs down tunnels. (This failure had been one of the reasons for the abrupt creation of human tunnel rats in 1966 after Operation Crimp.)

But the 25th was at war—and not just with an unseen enemy outside the wire. There was a fifth column inside as well, an enemy that found it easy

Camped on a volcano

COMBAT DOGS: "Nero," a US Army combat dog, and his handler searching for Viet Cong. At first the dogs were used to explore tunnels, but they triggered booby traps and there were so many canine casualties that the handlers refused to send them down— hence the need for human tunnel rats. Dogs continued to be used by US troops for above-ground operations.

to operate within the comparatively lax security system that took into account the entertainment needs of the soldiers and the necessity to use local labor to service the huge complex. The Vietnamese workers on the base lived in nearby strategic hamlets. In theory they were screened by the national police. In fact, some were guerrillas using tunnels around the base, and most workers were in touch with their local NLF organization. The Viet Cong cracked down heavily on fraternizing with the Americans, except on a commercial basis. For example, a Vietnamese girl who worked in the PX was known to be seeking permission to marry a GI. One morning

POSTHUMOUS CITATION: The Award for Outstanding Patriotism —the North Vietnamese equivalent of the Medal of Honor—made posthumously to Huynh Van Co. In 1966 he lived for a week in a tunnel under Cu Chi base, coming up each night and creating havoc. He was killed in 1969.

her head was found on a post outside the main gate, with note that said, "This is what happens to Vietnamese people who go around with the enemy." A special mobile punishment unit of Viet Cong was responsible for such executions.

The Vietnamese workers on Cu Chi base lined up to be counted and checked as they arrived and left each day. However, an explosive device or booby trap was found inside the base once or twice each week. Mess hall walls seemed to be a favorite place to leave them. One such bomb caused dozens of casualties in a mess hall on 5 January 1969. Today few of the civilian workers are happy to admit that they ever worked for the Americans. Mrs. Le Thi Tien, for example, is a self-employed seamstress with one child in the village of Phuoc Hiep, a short distance up Route 1, north of Cu Chi town. During the war she worked as a waitress in the officers' club on the base. She recalled: "I had to work there because my family was so poor. Most of the villages in this area were destroyed by bombs, so we all had to live temporarily in the villages along the road. I was forced to work for the Americans to support my mother, who was blind. I was told to observe everything in the base

94

and report it to the local cadre." The man to whom she reported was Ho Van Nhien, who is still the party cadre in Phuoc Hiep today. "Each village sent in spies," he said. "I had many report to me. Some were laborers filling sandbags. They reported whenever the Americans launched an operation. The bar girl (Mrs. Le Thi Tien) reported whenever she overheard conversations that she could understand. I reported back to the district committee so that they could prepare to deal with any attack." He described how intelligence messages detailing future search-and-destroy operations were written on small sheets of paper, wrapped in nylon, and hidden in the hair of women couriers, who attracted less suspicion from the police. Another of Ho's agents worked at the Graves registration point, the mortuary on Cu Chi base, preparing American dead for shipment home. By this means, the Viet Cong had a far more accurate picture of American casualty figures than was ever made public.

For attacks from outside, Cu Chi's intricate defensive perimeter turned out to be well justified. Not only did the Viet Cong lob mortar shells and rockets into Cu Chi base camp but, incredibly, they executed daring raids on it from the surrounding tunnels. These were carried out by parties of 30 or 40 guerrillas at most, and often by smaller groups, even by the classic Viet Cong three-man cells. Some caused enormous damage, to helicopters and tanks for example, and loss of life among the American soldiers. The raids were profoundly unsettling and of psychological and propaganda value far beyond their military importance. The Viet Cong demonstrated to the Americans that none of their installations was impregnable; that their adversaries were brave to the point of self-sacrifice; and that the Viet Cong would keep coming back, even after the annihilation of their villages and apparently fearsome casualties. Twenty years earlier, Ho Chi Minh, the North Vietnamese leader, had warned the French: "You can kill ten of my men for every one I kill of yours, but even at those odds, you will lose and I will win."

Once the Americans had succeeded in blocking up all the tunnels that ran underneath Cu Chi base, the Viet Cong created a complex structure of tunnels, trenches, and firing positions all around it. This

Ho Chi Minh —the North Vietnamese leader. He had warned the French colonialists: "You can kill ten of my men for every one I kill of yours, but even at those odds, you will lose and I will win."

ring of tunnels they called the belt. (The same technique had been used against the French at the siege of Dien Bien Phu in 1954.) The belt connected most of the villages surrounding Cu Chi base, including Trung Lap, Nhuan Duc, and Phu Hoa Dong. Every 50 meters, branch tunnels headed off toward the base itself. One set of branch tunnels ended in well-defended firing positions placed in the banks of the stream that ran along the northern side of Cu Chi base. The firing position that ended each branch tunnel was well concealed and surrounded by punji traps and mines. These nests of resistance commanded wide fields of fire and often overlooked, and hence dominated, one or another of the roads that crisscrossed the district. Because the branch tunnels led back into the main Cu Chi tunnel system, Viet Cong using firing positions to harass the enemy had a safe escape route when detected or shelled. The tunnels themselves had the multilevel structure that prevented damage from explosives or CS gas.

Viet Cong guerrilla Vo Thi Mo —she worked inside Cu Chi base as a spy and subsequently led Viet Cong guerrilla attacks upon it. She was a ruthless killer who softened long enough to let three GIs escape from her rifle sights.

The belt was constantly used for infiltration by main-force Viet Cong and from the more secure areas of War Zone C in Tay Ninh province or from Cambodia to attack Cu Chi base itself or to proceed to other attacks in or near Saigon.

One of those who worked and fought in the belt was Mrs. Vo Thi Mo, the one female guerrilla who survived the squad that stayed behind in Nhuan Duc. In 1966 she was still a teenager but dedicated to the cause she had espoused. "Our fighting area was the belt around Dong Zu (Cu Chi) base. My duty was to lead the way for the regular troops from Nhuan Duc to Dong Zu. In the daytime I went to Dong Zu openly by myself to observe the road, the fences, the terrain—the ways by which one could penetrate the base. Then at night I guided the reconnaissance group to observe the base. The regular forces mounted attacks. My duty was to guide the troops on their way back and help carry the wounded. Sometimes I went there legally, with puppet identity cards, on a Honda moped. Inside the base I was guided by liaison agents. I collected information from women inside the base, like cleaners and prostitutes, about the Americans' activities. I ran 15 secret cells. That way we knew in advance the names and times and places of some of the big operations, like Cedar Falls."

Camped on a volcano

FIGHTING ON THE BELT: Viet Cong guerrillas firing from the trench line that formed part of the belt of interconnecting tunnels and communication trenches that encircled Cu Chi base. All their rifles were captured from the Americans. The Viet Cong in the foreground has an M-14, the one next to him is aiming an M-1 carbine.

As late as February 1969, after three years of Cu Chi base's existence, the camp was the victim of a daring and destructive Viet Cong attack that penetrated right inside its security perimeter. It came from the least expected quarter: not from the notorious Ho Bo woods or Fil Hol sides, but from the side facing Cu Chi town, which was normally government controlled. Local guerrillas like Mrs. Mo had guided the Viet Cong main force around the belt to the side chosen for the attack. They slept the

Camped on a volcano

CAPTURED WEAPONS: In the early days of tunnel warfare, Viet Cong cells like this fought hard to acquire precious American weapons. These VC girl guerillas are wearing the classic black-and-white check scarves that identify them as members of the Viet Cong. The women were discouraged from hand-to-hand fighting with the physically larger GIs.

previous day in the tunnels. In the dead of night, Dac Cong, or special force, sappers crawled forward to clear a path through the protective minefield and barbed wire, unobserved by the patrolling sentries. Then the 39 Viet Cong, in three squads of 13, some of them women, entered the base. Their main aim, as with so many Viet Cong attacks, was to destroy their enemies' most feared and hated weapon—helicopters. They knew exactly where to find them. Using satchel charges, the guerillas blew up 14 of

LIFE BELOW:
A Viet Cong executive officer working below ground beneath a ventilation shaft. The shafts were specially constructed to provide light as well as air. The inscription on the wall is a typical Viet Cong poster of that era carrying an exhortation from Ho Chi Minh. It reads: "There is still an invader in the Vietnam territory. We have to continue to fight in order to sweep them out."

the big troop-carrying CH-47 Chinook helicopters on the ground, all those in Cu Chi at the time.

The realization that the Viet Cong were "inside the wire" created some panic. The defenders fired ghostly parachute flares into the air to illuminate the base and help spot the attackers. Firing broke out on all sides; there was the whoosh and boom of rocket grenades. A medical orderly in the 12th Evacuation Hospital later recalled that night: "Guys confirmed that the VC were inside the base. They said the enemy had killed some of our people and had blown up some helicopters. That the VC were inside our wire scared the wounded guys pretty bad. It scared me, too, and for the rest of the night, whenever the door opened on either ward my heart flipped and I froze, half expecting it would be VC. The shooting and the rockets and the flares kept up for hours."

Thirty-eight Americans were killed, but all but 13 of the attackers escaped safely and unharmed when they melted away before dawn. They left in a direction different from the one they had taken to reach the base; they knew that artillery fire would rake the area from which it was thought they had traveled.

By a cruel stroke of irony, the commander of the 25th Infantry at that time was Major General Ellis W. Williamson. He was the officer who had commanded the 173rd Airborne in 1966, and had been so scornful of the 25th's early tribulations with tunnels underneath the base. The destruction of so many helicopters during his command was, he said, heartbreaking.

CU CHI BASE TODAY:
The base is now empty and deserted. The gateway memorial was constructed after the war by the NVA using connecting pieces that were originally supplied to US forces for runway construction for light aircraft.

Operation Cedar Falls

BY 1967 the Americans were clearly having difficulties with the tunnels in Cu Chi. The Viet Cong
had so organized their local and regional forces that
not only did bases like Cu Chi face attack, but the
security of Saigon itself was threatened. General
Westmoreland had to address this growing problem.

Most of Cu Chi district was under ARVN or
American control by day, but the Viet Cong
dominated it by night. The guerrillas did not come
from empty air—they had to have shelter, food, and
weapons facilities. Many of these needs were supplied in the area adjoining Cu Chi, the large VC base
nearest to Saigon, which rejoiced in the menacing
name the Iron Triangle. For two years the
Americans treated the Triangle with respect and
caution, but in 1967 Westmoreland decided to mount
the largest and most destructive operation of the
war. He planned to take out the Iron Triangle and
its tunnels, to relieve the pressure on Saigon and
the surrounding bases, such as Cu Chi.

The Triangle was a 40-square-mile natural citadel
of jungle and briar, beneath which was a honeycomb
of Viet Cong tunnels and bunkers. Its apex was the
junction of the Saigon and Thi Tinh rivers, which
formed two of its sides. The third was an imaginary
line running from the village of Ben Suc eastward
to the district capital of Ben Cat. Like Cu Chi facing
it across the Saigon River, the Iron Triangle
dominated the strategic land and river routes into
Saigon.

Operation Cedar Falls (named after a town in
Iowa) was set for 8 January 1967. Its objects were
savage and uncompromising. First of all, the village
of Ben Suc was to be emptied of people and razed;
all the other villages in the Triangle would be

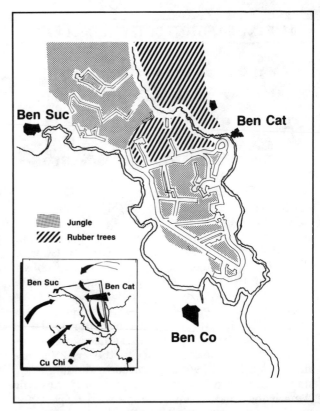

OPERATION CEDAR FALLS: US intelligence map showing the routes cleared by American troops during January 1967 as they swept through the Iron Triangle.

treated likewise. The chief aim of the operation was to locate the headquarters of the Viet Cong's Military Region IV (MR IV), explore it, and then destroy it, along with any other tunnels that were found. Once the civilian population had been cleared out of the Iron Triangle, it was to be stripped of vegetation and declared a free strike zone.

A week of softening-up bombing missions by B-52s preceded the operation. The Vietnam War had begun as a counterinsurgency war—stalking guerrillas in the jungle. Cedar Falls, however, was a multidivisional operation involving 30,000 US troops, the largest in Vietnam to date.

On 8 January 1967 the village of Ben Suc—former population about 3,500—was wiped off the face of the earth. Its subsequent survival and rebirth testify to the importance of the tunnels in frustrating America's aims in Operation Cedar Falls, and in the

Vietnam War as a whole. As long as the tunnels were not eliminated, neither were the spirit and effectiveness of the guerrillas.

Ben Suc was strategically situated at the crossing point of the Saigon River, on the northern bank facing Phu My Hung in Cu Chi district; it was the western point of the Iron Triangle. Because the Americans assumed that approaches to Ben Suc would be mined and booby trapped, and that a battalion of Viet Cong would be defending the village, a new form of attack was planned. An entire battalion, 500 men of the 1st/26th Infantry, the "Blue Spaders," commanded by a future secretary of state and presidential candidate, Lieutenant Colonel Alexander M. Haig, were airlifted into the middle of the village by 60 UH-1 helicopters.

There was no significant resistance in Ben Suc; the only American casualties were caused by booby trap mines. The village was sealed and secured, and in a short while a battalion of the ARVN was helicoptered in to search the village and interrogate the inhabitants. That same day, all the men in the village between 15 and 45 were flown out in Chinooks for further interrogation at the provincial police headquarters. Those thought not to be Viet

BLUE SPADERS: Gen. William Westmoreland decorates Lt. Col. Alexander Haig, who later became a US secretary of state. Haig's battalion, the Blue Spaders of the 1st/26th Infantry, led the assault on Ben Suc. Its civilian population was sent to the "safety" of strategic hamlets. But when they had gone the tunnel fighters stayed.

Operation Cedar Falls

HQ UNCOVERED: Brig. Gen. Richard T. Knowles (left) at the entrance to a Viet Cong tunnel headquarters discovered by men of his 196th Infantry Brigade during Cedar Falls. The 196th's haul included maps, detailed plans, weapons, and booby traps inside the 600 yards of tunnels they penetrated. Platoon Sgt. James Lindsay (center) keeps in telephone contact with his men inside the tunnel network. He was killed a couple of days later by a booby trap as he explored further into the complex.

Cong would be inducted into the South Vietnamese Army. The next day, all the remaining villagers were shipped out, with whatever belongings they could carry and such animals as they could round up.

When the last truckload of people and boatload of animals had left Ben Suc, the demolition teams moved in. The grass-roofed houses were soaked in gasoline and razed, leaving spindly black frames, charred furniture, and the entrances to bomb shelters. Then the bulldozers went to work, flattening all the more solid buildings, fences, and graveyards. Afterwards 1st Division engineers stacked 10,000 pounds of explosives and 1,000 gallons of napalm in a crater in the center of the ruined village, covered them with earth, and tamped it all down with bulldozers. A chemical fuse triggered the 5-ton explosion; it was hoped that it would blast any undiscovered tunnels in the vicinity. "One of the major objectives of Cedar Falls had been achieved," wrote General Bernard Rogers of the 1st Infantry Division. "The village of Ben Suc no longer existed."

Maj. Gen. Bernard Rogers —deputy commander of the 1st Infantry Division at the time of Cedar Falls. It was not the success anticipated. After the operation he wrote, "it was not long before there was evidence of the enemy's return to the Iron Triangle."

But that was just the overture to Cedar Falls. The bulk of the American troops were to be thrown into the rest of the Iron Triangle. By the end of the first day, an entire American corps had moved into position along its sides. At dawn on 9 January, this mighty leviathan stirred and rolled into action.

As the operation began, the 196th Light Infantry swept through the tunnel-riddled Ho Bo woods in Cu Chi. At first all they achieved was "the uncovering of a small quantity of enemy supplies." Brigadier General Richard T. Knowles realized he had to devise a way of finding well-camouflaged tunnel entrances as a matter of urgency; tunnel detection would be vital to the conduct of Cedar Falls. He had a bright idea. He had vehicles, such as APCs, drag whole trees behind them through the woods, creating avenues of swept dust as clear as virgin snow. "Then in the morning," he said, "we could see where the VC had come out of their holes, and how they got back. You could see where they crawled, and where they stood up and ran. One thing led to another and we found the openings." These early tunnel finds would lead to more substantial success later in the three-week operation.

Other units, too, were finding tunnels. After the

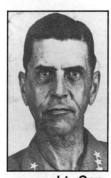

Lt. Gen. Jonathan O. Seaman —as commander of II Field Force he was in overall control of Cedar Falls. He claimed that he had turned the Iron Triangle into a "military desert."

occupation of Ben Suc, 1st Infantry Division engineers began flattening the nearby jungle with bulldozers. Their commanding officer, Lieutenant Colonel Joseph M. Kiernan (who was to die in a helicopter crash in June 1967) recalled at the time: "I guess it was about 20 acres of scrub jungle . . . The place was so infested with tunnels that as my dozers would knock over the stumps of trees, the VC would pop out from behind the dozers. We captured about . . . six or eight VC one morning. They just popped out of the tunnels and we picked them up."

Other Big Red One battalions were helicopter-lifted into the Thanh Dien forest north of Ben Suc. The Thanh Dien was known as a Viet Cong rest-and-resupply area, but most of the guerrillas had wisely melted away and there was little resistance. Indeed, some troops reported seeing "an unknown number of Viet Cong escaping south on bicycles." Tunnels, bunkers, and rice caches were uncovered, and a significant find was made by the 1st Battalion, 28th Infantry. After coming under fire from a Viet Cong unit that killed four GIs and wounded four, Company B of the battalion came across a huge underground medical complex, containing over a ton of medicine, much of it bought in Saigon. The defenders had held off the "Black Lions" of the 1st Infantry Division until all the wounded guerrillas could be evacuated. The fighters had in fact been a scratch squad of pharmacists commanded by a doctor, Vo Hoang Le. They, too, melted back into the jungle.

The Army came closest to the real objective of Cedar Falls on 18 January, ten days after the operation began. Tunnel rats from the 1st/5th Infantry—the "Bobcats"—under Captain Bill Pelfrey discovered an extensive tunnel complex beside the Rach Son stream, which flows into the Saigon River from the middle of Cu Chi district. The tunnels were beneath the narrow strip of open land between the Fil Hol plantation to the south and the Ho Bo woods. Thousands of documents were discovered, which were taken away in sacks by helicopter. The rats spent four days exploring the winding galleries of the system.

For the 196th, the haul was impressive. In addition to the sacks of documents, there was a typewriter, furniture, women's clothing (including brassieres and *ao dais*, traditional costume), Viet Cong flags, and other indications that the tunnels were part of a headquarters. The half-million documents, once translated, yielded information that led Lieutenant General Jonathan Seaman (who was in overall command) to call the find "the biggest intelligence breakthrough of the war." Among other discoveries there was some "crypto-material"—coded messages that could help unlock other intelligence intercepts. There were detailed maps of the Saigon area and Tan Son Nhut air base, including the plans for an unsuccessful Viet Cong attack that had taken place a month earlier.

Brigadier General Richard Knowles hurried to the scene of the discovery. He remembered that the documents "showed how they moved squads down from Cambodia into the Cu Chi area, and then down to Tan Son Nhut. It showed where they stayed in the tunnels during the daylight, and where they collected their weapons. They had the parking places of all our aircraft laid out in detail. Even the symbols for the aircraft looked like the real things. Everything was numbered in logical sequence: when each gun was to fire, how many mortar rounds, how many rockets—a classic! In addition to that we found a map with considerable detail, showing where they'd planned to ambush and kill Secretary of Defense Robert McNamara in the middle of Saigon." (The plot, in mid-1966, had been frustrated by a change in the target's schedule; the intended assassin, Nguyen Van Troi, was arrested and executed.) In the same pile of documents were lists of addresses of prominent Americans in Saigon, including General Westmoreland. Bill Pelfrey, who led the exploration, said: "The biggest part was tax receipts dating back 20 years. There were lists of their sympathizers—who needed political training, or punishment or whatever. They had American technical manuals translated into Vietnamese."

Because the find was regarded as such a major coup, General Westmoreland himself was helicoptered into the area to talk with the tunnel rats, accompanied by other VIPs, reporters, and television crews—even though there were still booby traps in the tunnels, and some VC hiding in recesses in the system. The tunnel rats pursued them, but gave up after crawling over a thousand yards. The

Brig. Gen. Richard T. Knowles —during Cedar Falls he had vehicles drag trees across the dusty landscape, creating avenues of swept dust as clear as virgin snow. The next morning US troops could see the footprints left behind by the Viet Cong who had emerged from the tunnels under cover of darkness. Knowles' idea proved an effective method for detecting tunnel entrances.

In the photo sign:
CAPTURED BY
THE IRON BRIGADE
OPERATION
"CEDAR FALLS"
ẢN 3 TICH.THU ĐƯỢC TRONG
H.QUAN "CEDAR FALLS"

senior NCO on the team, Sergeant James Lindsay, was killed underground by an explosive booby trap. Once Pelfrey decided that no more of the system was worth exploring, it was filled with CS gas, then blasted with explosives.

No official conclusion was reached as to the real status of the tunnel complex the 196th Light Infantry had stumbled across. Because of the volume of documents discovered, General Bernard Rogers believed that "this discovery probably uncovered the headquarters of Military Region IV, or at least a significant part of it." In fact, Cedar Falls missed that target, and the police headquarters of the Viet Cong for the Saigon area as well; they were both slightly farther north in the Ho Bo woods. The area of the tunnel that had been found and destroyed is today clearly marked on maps and records at the Ho Chi Minh City military headquarters. It was the Viet Cong's headquarters for the Cu Chi district only. Escape tunnels are shown to have burrowed away from it southward.

By the time of Cedar Falls, the tunnel rats in various units were refining techniques of exploration and destruction. The problem in that operation was that because tunnels were discovered so often, too many untrained and inexperienced men went underground. Consequently, there were mishaps that resulted in "noncombat" deaths. A private in the 4th/503rd Infantry, for example, suffocated to death on 22 January because an earlier grenade explosion had burned up all the oxygen in a tunnel. Several ad hoc tunnel rats lost their bearings and came up to the surface completely lost. On one occasion two separate tunnel teams were exploring the same system independently and only good luck prevented their shooting at each other underground. Cedar Falls had the effect of establishing tunnel-ratting as a skilled specialty, and the rats would be better organized in the future.

When the operation ended, and the troops quit the operational area to return to their bases, their commanders assessed what they had achieved. As usual in Vietnam, the brightest possible picture was painted in the after-action reports. Lieutenant General Seaman reported at the time: "In 19 days, II Field Force Vietnam converted the Iron Triangle from a safe haven to a deathtrap, and then to a

PROPAGANDA II: A Viet Cong guerrilla chalks political graffiti on the back of a destroyed US armored personnel carrier. The slogan reads: "Johnson's dollars are the blood and tears of the American soldiers."

military desert. Years of work spent tunneling and hoarding supplies were nullified. . . . A strategic enemy base was decisively engaged and destroyed." Unfortunately, this was just wishful thinking.

General Westmoreland reached a more modest and realistic verdict. He called Cedar Falls "very disruptive . . . for the enemy in the Iron Triangle area." The evidence suggests that this was the limit of its success—temporary disruption. At the provincial headquarters of the newly created province of Song Be, which covers what used to be the Iron Triangle, the authors were shown a hitherto secret Vietnamese army report entitled "Lessons of the War." The US Army claimed 525 tunnels destroyed during Cedar Falls. But Major Nguyen Quot, who was assigned by the commander of the Viet Cong Military Region IV to assess the damage, said: "After the operation I inspected the tunnels and did not find any length more than 50 meters that had been discovered or damaged by the Americans. They had destroyed only about 100 tunnels with explosives, and a lot of civilians' bomb shelters." Every house in Ben Suc, for example, had an underground shelter connected by tunnel to other shelters. Naturally, most of these were collapsed, inflating the statistics of tunnels destroyed.

Pham Van Chinh —commander of the Viet Cong guerrillas at Ben Suc. He stayed in the tunnels while US forces flattened his village.

Worse still, just two days after Cedar Falls, General Rogers witnessed the failure of one of the operation's main objectives: denying the area to the enemy. "It was not long before there was evidence of the enemy's return. Only two days after the termination of Cedar Falls, I was checking out the Iron Triangle by helicopter and saw many persons who appeared to be Viet Cong riding bicycles or wandering round on foot. . . . During the cease-fire for Tet, 8-12 February, the Iron Triangle was again literally crawling with what appeared to be Viet Cong. They could be seen riding into, out of, and within the Triangle."

Even the depopulation of Ben Suc had failed. Incredibly the village's Viet Cong commander, Pham Van Chinh, and many of his guerrillas remained clinging to the land as they had been ordered. They hid in part of the village's 1,700-meter tunnel system, much of which had survived despite the discovery and destruction of three of its entrances during Cedar Falls.

Acetylene gas and water from the river had been pumped into the tunnels, but they were complex and multileveled enough to ensure the safety of those guerrillas who had not fallen victim to the first wave of the assault. "When the people were taken away," said Chinh, "it was difficult for us. The people had been supporting the guerrillas, their sons and brothers. The destruction of the people's houses caused my bitter hatred. The enemy turned the land into a desert. There was not a tree left. But I could still count on over 200 men to fight beside me during the Cedar Falls operation." Chinh's orders were to lie low and wait for the Americans' inevitable departure before repairing the tunnel system. Through Viet Cong couriers, he made contact with the displaced villagers. Although Ben Suc and the rest of the Triangle was henceforth a free strike zone, with bombs and shells regularly falling upon it, the villagers began to trickle back to their ancestral land.

By the end of the year, over a thousand villagers
had drifted back to Ben Suc. As the guerrillas
reconstructed the tunnels so necessary for bringing
main-force Viet Cong from Cambodia down to the
Iron Triangle, Cu Chi, and Saigon itself, so the
returning villagers lived in their old bomb shelters
or dug new chambers and tunnels, some shared by
families. Grass grew on top of these refuges, conceal-
ing them from view.

But the most conclusive demonstration of the in-

Operation Cedar Falls

SWEEPING THE FOREST: Troops and tanks search the Thanh Dien Forest just north of the Iron Triangle. It had hitherto been a Viet Cong sanctuary. It was here that they discovered a huge underground hospital complex. A USD general helicoptered in called it "one ginormous medical depot."

effectiveness of Cedar Falls and the search-and-destroy operations like it came almost exactly one year later.

The Tet lunar new year festival of 1968 would see a countrywide series of Viet Cong attacks on bases and towns, including Saigon, that threw the Americans off balance and marked the beginning of the end of their involvement in Vietnam. And the most damaging thrust—that against Saigon itself—would come straight from the Iron Triangle.

115

Operation Cedar Falls

CARVED IN THE JUNGLE: One of the bulldozers equipped with a Rome Plow blade—known as hogjaws—that were used to strip 80-yard-wide avenues across the Iron Triangle. VC tunnel fighters caught by the plows while hiding in the bushes were sliced to pieces. INSET: Seen from the air the insignia of the Ist Infantry Division (bottom) and the US Army Engineers (a huge castle) that were carved by bulldozers during Cedar Falls.

Rat Six and Batman

THE SPECIAL IMPORTANCE of the tunnels was acknowledged by the Americans as their military presence in Vietnam reached its peak—to over half a million men by mid-1968. If some lessons in tunnel warfare remained unlearned, Cedar Falls had at least one noticeable result: the decision not to allow untrained men to explore tunnels. There had been too many "noncombat" deaths underground. After that operation, the commander of the only division with an organized tunnel rat team—the Big Red One—transferred that role from his chemical platoon to the engineers, who were expert in demolition explosives. In June 1967, the Tunnel Rat team was formally created as an offshoot of the intelligence and reconnaissance section of the 1st Engineer Battalion. A lieutenant commanded the team, and he was known as Rat Six, "six" being the division's own code word for a commander.

Rat Six was supported by one or two sergeants. Sergeant Robert Batten was assigned to the rats from the outset and then volunteered for two extra tours of duty, staying in Vietnam for three years. Universally known as Batman, he was the most feared and respected of the tunnel rats. He was from New Jersey, a red-haired man in his mid-twenties. It was he, not the officers, who was credited with the elite reputation that the rat squad came to enjoy. During his time, the team could boast a body count of over 100 enemy dead.

First, last, and foremost, tunnel rats were individualists. If Batten was uneasy with a volunteer, the man would never be appointed. There were many Hispanics, though; one officer called them "Napoleon types." Most of the men had months of experience in Vietnam before volunteering for the

Tunnel life —the bamboo viper *Trimeresurus popeorum.* "They weren't very long, but they had a very potent bite; once bitten you could only take one or two more steps."—Lt. Jack Flowers, also known as Rat Six.

rat squad, and would serve only a year in total. The officers rotated even more frequently; the average Rat Six served four months. The team was about seven or eight men strong, except for the short period in 1969 when there were two tunnel rat teams. The men received an extra $50 a month as hazardous-duty pay. Each team had its own medic and radio operator, and there were two long-serving Kit Carson scouts, Tiep and Hien.

Kit Carson scouts (named after the hero of the Old West) were men who had defected from the Viet Cong in return for a promise of clemency from the South Vietnamese. American infantry platoons came increasingly to depend upon them. They could instinctively assess dangerous situations that young, green, and annually-rotated GIs would have stumbled into and discovered the hard way. They had local knowledge, spoke the language, and were intimately familiar with Viet Cong methods. They could communicate with prisoners, villagers, and the ARVN troops. Trained as soldiers, and properly fed and looked after, they added to the strength of American rifle platoons, depleted by soldiers going sick, being wounded, or taking rest and recreation.

The tunnel rats were particular beneficiaries of the Kit Carson scouts who had often worked in the tunnels in their Viet Cong days. They knew the probable layout of any tunnel system and the likely

TUNNEL TEAM: The Tunnel Rats of the 1st Engineer Battalion based at Lai Khe. Left and second from right are the Kit Carson scouts, Tiep and Hien. They all wear the tunnel badge on their right breast pockets. Only tunnel rats were allowed to wear jungle hats— like the Viet Cong they fought.

location of booby traps. They undertook the task of coaxing cornered VC or NVA out. They were full-time and served continuously. As a result, any one of them soon acquired more experience in tunnel warfare from the American side than the members of the teams they assisted, where the personnel changed constantly with the annual rotation system. But they were never completely trusted.

Lieutenant Jack Flowers was Rat Six from February to August 1969. He was a college dropout from Indiana who had been drafted. He was short, tough, and spiky, with an aggressive crewcut and a prominent, jutting lower jaw. Once in the Army, he was sent to Officer Candidate School. After a few short assignments in the United States, he arrived in Vietnam as a second lieutenant in the Corps of Engineers. He was assigned as a platoon leader to the 1st Engineer Battalion at Lai Khe. Flowers's first tasks were supervising the cutting down of trees and the clearing of landing zones, and similar duties. A few weeks later on, he was bitterly stung to be called a "REMF" (rear echelon motherfucker) by a helicopter pilot he had kept waiting, and who taunted him: "I've got to pick up some guys who've been fighting all day." Another officer explained the term REMF to Flowers. He knew it was the (usually welcome) fate of the great many Americans who served in Vietnam—to be part of the huge tail of logistics and support units that kept a relatively small number of unfortunate grunts in actual combat. Flowers was planning to become a total REMF, an information officer at divisional headquarters at Di An, when unexpectedly he was invited to volunteer to become Rat Six—in his words, "the worst and most dangerous job in the battalion" for an officer. He suddenly saw the war anew. He remembered seeing a dead grunt being dragged messily out of a tunnel two weeks before and felt a surge of militancy. He was being asked to join the war. No one would ever call him a REMF again. To his own amazement, he accepted.

That night he ate dinner with the battalion S-2, or intelligence officer, a captain. Flowers recalled the very words of the briefing: "You're only going to have one problem, Jack, and that's Batman."

"Batman? I thought he was the whole key to the rats."

The sign that hung on the door of the 1st Engineer Battalion Tunnel Rats' "hootch" at Lai Khe base. They saw themselves as hard-drinking, mean-mouthed, fast-shooting sons of bitches. The reverse was true. They were cool, calculating, and ruthless.

Rat Six and Batman

HOT JOB:
Tunnel rats
from the 25th
Infantry digging
in a collapsed
tunnel toward
a Viet Cong
underground
grenade factory
in Cu Chi. The
claustrophobic
conditions
meant that all
tunnel rats
were
volunteers.
They earned an
additional $50
a month for
"hazardous
duty."

"He is. That's the problem. He knows it, too. On the surface he's like any other NCO, pretty good-natured, keeps his men straight, respects rank and everything else. But he's different inside. Nobody in his right mind should love being a tunnel rat, but he does. Your biggest job is going to be to learn everything he knows and yet still be in charge. There's a rule with the rats: there's no rank underground. Don't try to be a hero. They know what has to be done, and Batman is very proud of the fact that none of the rats has ever been killed."

"How many have been wounded?"

The captain laughed. "I think he's proud of that

fact, too. Everybody's been wounded at least once."

The next day Flowers was introduced to the formidable Batman, the man who had voluntarily stayed in Vietnam three times longer than necessary. Flowers remembered their conversation, too: Why had the sergeant stayed in-country for so long?

"Because I love getting those gooks out of there. They think they have it made down there in those holes. Well, they've got it made like a rat's ass when Batman comes after 'em."

Wasn't two years of war enough for anybody?

"Not if it's the only one you've got." He looked

THE HUMAN PROBE: Tunnel Rat Sgt. Pete Rejo in action. He was one of the meanest, working alone, hating and killing the Communist fighters in their holes. His squad called him the Human Probe. "I loved it down there...when they told me they had a VC down there, I came unglued."

knowingly at the lieutenant. "We'll get along just fine if you stay out of my way. Otherwise you might get hurt and I'd have to be dragging you out feet first. I got more important things to do. So just stay out of my way."

But unlike some of his predecessors, this Rat Six wanted to lead his squad underground himself, and never ask an enlisted man to do anything he would not do. In other words, he intended to command the tunnel rats in fact as well as theory, to take over the role that had hitherto been Sergeant Batten's. He decided that Batman could remain the undisputed leader of the squad for the next 30 days only. After that, Flowers would have learned enough to take over.

Then he met the rats. They wore clean, pressed uniforms and well-shined boots. Above their breast pockets they wore the tunnel rat badge with its nonsense Latin motto, "Not worth a rat's ass." Flowers was given one of the badges on the strength of having been in a tunnel once since he had been in Vietnam. For most grunts the Vietnam War was an uncomfortable and indecisive business of counting the days of one's year in-country. Flowers sensed immediately that the rats were different. Volunteers for a hazardous assignment, they were well-motivated professionals with codes and rules of their own, which Flowers would have to honor.

Assiduous training then followed for the young officer. One skill to be learned, in a specially converted culvert, was hand-to-hand fighting on hands and knees. There were rules about operating in tunnels. You would never fire off more than three shots from your revolver in the darkness; fire off six and an enemy would know you were out of ammunition. Week by week, Flowers began to chalk up tunnel missions and experience.

By March 1969 the enemy was back in the Iron Triangle, and on the 26th, the tunnel rats were called out again by Colonel George Patton, son of General George Patton of World War II fame. North Vietnamese army soldiers had been spotted disappearing into a tunnel complex after a fierce battle beside the Saigon River. One of Patton's tank commanders followed them into the tunnel and was immediately killed by a booby trap.

When Flowers and the team arrived, Batman took one man with him into the tunnel. Flowers heard shots and grenade explosions down below, and minutes later Batman appeared at the bottom of the entrance shaft, announcing that the other rat was wounded. They dragged the man, bleeding from shrapnel wounds in his arms and legs, up to the surface. Then Batman's head peered out. "The pricks have got us cold," he reported. "They're sitting on top of a trapdoor." Flowers asked the sergeant what he advised, and Batman said they should go back after the NVA. To Batman's slight surprise, Flowers himself insisted on coming down; Batman, in Flowers's view, had won enough medals already, and it was one of Flowers's men who had been wounded.

Flowers entered the tunnel, and followed Batman to the first sealed trapdoor in the roof. Smoke and fumes hung in the air from the grenade that had wounded the first tunnel rat. Batman cautiously pushed the trapdoor upward, then quickly fired three shots into the blackness. Then he took his lamp and put his head through the hole. "Give me

Tunnel life —the black-bearded tomb bat *taphozous solifer.* "Sometimes you'd be scared and open fire and the bats started coming out through the tunnel. One bat grabbed a man in the groin area, and just bit him, and he took his .38 and blew him away." —S.Sgt. Rick Swofford, 1st Engineers Battalion tunnel rat.

your pistol," he commanded Flowers. Flowers passed
it up and started reloading Batman's. One NVA
soldier hiding in the tunnel had retreated; it could
turn into a long pursuit. Batman went ahead and
soon came across another trapdoor leading down-
ward. Flowers followed a few yards behind, the distance beyond which a grenade explosion would not
be lethal. Batman approached the new trapdoor in
the same way. He lifted it and started firing. Suddenly an automatic weapon lashed out from underneath. Dirt flew everywhere. Batman fell backward.
Flowers assumed that he'd been hit. He crawled up

Rat Six and Batman

RAT SIX AND BATMAN: Lt. Jack Flowers (center), also known as Rat Six, is congratulated by Maj. Gen. Orwin Talbott, commander of the Big Red One, on receipt of his bronze star. "Batman," Sgt. Robert Batten, is on the right. Later Batman was to warn his officer: "You're not a killer...and that's your problem ...you'll screw up somewhere." He was right. Eventually Flowers was ordered back to the States after one nightmare operation.

to the sergeant. Batman was unhurt, but dirt had been thrown into his face and gone into his eyes. Flowers crawled up to him and Batman indicated the small 12-by-12-inch opening. "Shoot in there," he said. Flowers fired three shots and reloaded as Batman sat rubbing his eyes, talking to himself, psyching himself up for the continued pursuit. "Those pricks. Here they are, trying to kill me again." He tried to move past Flowers. "You've had your two trapdoors," said the lieutenant. (The rule was that the point man would be changed after two trapdoors, so great was the stress and tension.) Bat

127

Rat Six and Batman

DANGEROUS DESCENT:
A tunnel rat is lowered into a tunnel in order to survey the complex before planting explosives. This photograph is one of many pictures of tunnel rats that the Vietnamese Communists displayed in their museums that commemorate the war.

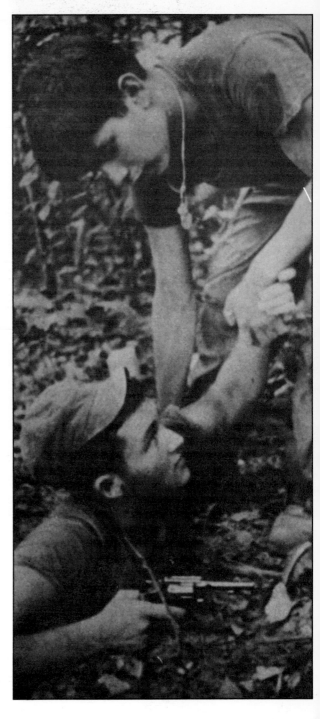

man looked at him groggily, six inches from his face, and conceded. Flowers edged past Batman, and went down through the trapdoor.

He fired three more shots as he crawled down to the lower level, and three more from Batman's pistol as he approached a curve in the tunnel on his knees, flashlight in one hand, gun in the other. Batman came down behind him. The tunnel straightened out, then went another 10 yards and stopped at a wall. A little dirt fell from the ceiling at the end, betraying the existence of a rectangular trapdoor to another level up. Flowers held his lamp steadily on the door.

The NVA soldier was evidently lying just over the trapdoor. Batman moved up beside Flowers and made to push upward on it. But Flowers prevented him. Flowers was Rat Six, and the point man; he insisted upon dealing with the situation by himself. Batman crawled back a few yards. Flowers tensed in apprehension; sweat was running into his eyes. He edged up to the wall and sat under the trapdoor about 12 inches above his head. He placed a lamp between his legs, shining upward. Then he put his hand under the door and exerted a small amount of pressure. Batman cocked his pistol; Flowers gripped his. Flowers took a deep breath of the dank air and pushed up on the door. It yielded. He twisted it and set it down crosswise on its beveled frame. Then he paused, planning to slide it away and start firing into the void.

A foot above Flowers's glistening and grimy face, the trapdoor was quietly turned round and slotted back into its frame. Flowers froze; the gook was right there. Suddenly the door moved again. Something dropped into Flowers's lap, right in front of his eyes. He watched it fall, momentarily transfixed; then the danger to his life overwhelmed him as he screamed "Grenade!"

The American M-26 grenade has a steel casing over a coil of pressed steel. The coil is designed to burst into over 700 pieces, and the case into chunks of shrapnel. It is fatal at up to 5 meters. It is detonated when the pin is pulled that releases a handle, igniting the fuse. The acid fuse burns for five to seven seconds before the detonator sets off the pound of high explosive.

In his nightmares for years afterward, Jack Flowers saw that grenade falling as a series of still

Tunnel life —Scorpion *chactidae euscorpius.* "In the Cu Chi tunnels the VC used to take boxes of scorpions with a tripwire and that was a booby trap. You tripped the wire, the box would open, and the scorpions would come into the tunnel. One of my men got stung; he came out screaming and never went back into another tunnel." —Lt. Jack Flowers.

frames in a slowed-up reel of film, dropping jerkily, hypnotically. . . .

Flowers did not know how far he had crawled when the explosion ripped through the tunnel. There was a tremendous ringing in his ears and his legs were bleeding, but he was still crawling. Batman, too, was moving away when Flowers reached him. He shone his lamp on Flowers's torn and bloody fatigues. Flowers was suddenly preoccupied about having dropped his pistol. Batman advised him to forget it and keep moving. Another explosion rocked

the tunnel. The NVA soldier was trying to make sure that the tunnel rats were dead, even pursuing them. Flowers blindly scrambled back through the different levels. When at last he saw daylight, and reached for the hands of the men above, he collapsed. When he came round, medics were taking shrapnel out of wounds in his legs. Colonel George Patton was standing over him.

The exit to the tunnel was under one of Patton's tanks; the NVA had been trapped. But Flowers decided against further pursuit. Tiep, the Kit Car

TRACER SHOT: Holding a flashlight, a tunnel rat fires a tracer bullet. In the inky darkness of the tunnels, the bullet's trajectory can be followed.

on scout, tried to talk the NVA soldiers out, without success. Charges were set at each tunnel entrance timed to go off simultaneously and cave in the whole structure. Batman, like Flowers, already had a ruptured eardrum from the earlier grenade explosions. As the dust-off helicopter took them off to hospital, the tunnel collapsed; the enemy was smothered to death. Next day Colonel Patton ordered the bodies to be dug up for body count.

Flowers recalled his thoughts in the hospital bed. "If it had been John Wayne, he would have picked up the grenade, lifted up the trapdoor, and thrown it back at the bastards. If it had been Audie Murphy, he would have thrown his body over the grenade to save Batman's life, and his mother would have received his posthumous Medal of Honor. But since it was Jack Flowers, I started crawling like hell." In fact, both men received The Bronze Star (V) from the division's commanding general. For all his self-preservation instinct, Flowers had been blooded underground. At last he was Batman's equal.

The fifteenth of May, 1969, was Sergeant Robert Batten's DEROS—date of estimated return from overseas. He was not allowed to extend, or take another tour. He wanted to carry on killing gooks,

but the decision was taken at divisional level to send him home. He had been wounded four times, and twice was the normal limit. Flowers sat drinking with Batman for some hours a few days before the sergeant left Vietnam. Batman delivered his verdict on the lieutenant. Flowers had been determined to emulate the sergeant's toughness and courage. Batman was not deceived; he made a scornful prediction. "You're not a killer, Six, and that's your problem. You're pretty good, the best Six I ever had, but you'll fuck up somewhere. Charlie hasn't killed a rat for quite a time. And you'll either let him get you, or what's worse, you'll get yourself."

Flowers heard that Batman left the army when his final request to return to Vietnam was turned down; he returned to New Jersey to work on construction sites. The new sergeant was Peter Schultz. He was a good NCO and demolitions man, but solidly built and over 6 feet tall—the wrong physique for a rat. He was reliant on Flowers's tunnel knowledge. Without Batman, Flowers was exposed; it was as if he had lost his right arm, the ultimate source of tun

TUNNEL STRESS: An exhausted sergeant being treated by a medic after spending several hours searching a tunnel complex in the Iron Triangle. Many tunnel rats' nerves gave way underground. Once it happened, they were never sent down tunnels again.

nel wisdom and know-how. Increased work and responsibility weighed upon Flowers. He led mission after mission, but fatigue began to infect him, and with it, fear. In one tunnel the enemy set off a large mine that completely buried him. It took Sergeant Schultz five minutes to dig him out, unconscious.

The end came in late July 1969. Flowers and the rats were on a mission in the Iron Triangle that discovered a Viet Cong base camp in the course of construction, with woven baskets and long bamboo poles to hoist the earth from the tunnels. The rats explored a succession of holes into which Viet Cong

Rat Six and Batman

FIND AND DESTROY:
An explosive charge shatters part of a tunnel complex near Tuy Hoa. Frequently these huge explosions created only localized damage in the tunnel system. Usually the Viet Cong were able to repair or bypass the damaged section within a few days. INSET: Explosive kit consisting of a "Steel Pot," demolition cord, blasting caps, and large quantities of C-4 plastic explosives.

or NVA had run to hide when the 1st/4th Cavalry had arrived in the area. All proved to be cold. At length only one hole remained. And all the soldiers in the tunnel rat squad knew that at least one enemy had to be down there. Flowers realized that every member of the squad had been down a tunnel that day except him. Sergeant Schultz offered to take one of the Kit Carson scouts and explore the last hole. But Flowers knew that as the officer in charge, he had to take the most dangerous job himself. As usual, a grenade was dropped down the shaft first, but all the rats were aware that this was little

**Tunnel life —giant crab spider *heteropoda venatoria*. "...for a moment I thought I was losing my equilibrium because it seemed like the hole was moving in on me, and as I shined the light round more, I found out it was just a mass of spiders—just these spiders. The whole chamber, the walls and the top, were one great black moving mass of spiders."
—M.Sgt. Robert Baer.**

more than a noisy warning gesture. The Viet Cong had years of experience ducking around corners in tunnels to avoid the very limited range of a grenade.

The hole was about 15 feet deep, and curved away to one side at the bottom. Flowers knew that it was not connected to any of the other holes, so if his theory was right, the Viet Cong had to be down there, waiting for him. He sent for a Swiss seat, a cradle of straps in which he could be lowered into a hole. The two strongest men would pay out the rope to lower Flowers to a point 3 feet from the bottom, then at a signal suddenly drop him, to surprise the waiting Viet Cong. It could take 30 seconds to get down. Flowers assessed the situation coolly: The only question to be answered was survival at the other end. It would be a confrontation that he had long anticipated. The rest of his squad looked at him grimly. As Flowers went over the side of the hole, the two Kit Carson scouts were almost tearful, the newer tunnel rats appalled by the ordeal. Schultz offered the lieutenant a second pistol. Flowers declined it, but ordered that it be ready loaded to drop down to him. If they heard anything other than his pistol firing, they were to pull him up.

Flowers began his suspended descent. Fear gripped him, the fear that knows no ranks and possesses every young man who faces the reality that his life might be stolen from him in a few, fleeting seconds. As Lieutenant Flowers thought back over his life, the image of Batman kept reappearing to him, saying, "You'll fuck up, you'll fuck up." His feet and elbows rubbed against the sides of the shaft, dislodging clods of earth that would tell the Viet Cong below that he was coming down. Flowers pictured the enemy down there on his knees, leaning against the side of the tunnel with his AK-47 set on full automatic fire. In an aperture about four feet in diameter it would be hard to miss. Twenty rounds would cut through Flowers in four seconds. So Flowers knew that the first shot from his pistol would have to kill the VC. He would aim straight at the VC's face; a shot to the body would not disable him enough to prevent him firing the AK-47. Flowers swung sideways, with his arm over his chest and his right shoulder hunched to protect his temple, to minimize the wounds he was bound to take. He was 3 feet from the tunnel floor. He signaled to Schultz to release the rope. The moment had come. Flowers hit the floor with his pistol firing; the first shot went through the VC's forehead, the second his cheek, the third his throat, the fourth and fifth and sixth pounded into his body. Blood racing to his brain, Flowers kept pulling the trigger, clicking on the empty chambers of his revolver. Schultz heard the firing and instantly hurled the loaded pistol down to his Rat Six. The gun clattered down the shaft.

The smell of cordite lingered in the dank tunnel air.

Flowers stared dumbly in front of him, disbelieving what his mind had created. There was no enemy soldier there, no adversary with a rifle, just a blank wall with six holes neatly grouped in the earth. Six. And the time-honored law of the tunnel rats said no more than three. Sergeant Schultz and the others peered down at their leader. The Rat Six had faced his enemy. Somewhere inside Flowers's head, Batman laughed.

Two days later at Lai Khe the battalion's executive officer relieved Flowers of his tunnel rat command, and told him to go home. "Don't make me tell you what you already know. You're finished. You've fought your war. Stay out of sight for three weeks, then forget all about Vietnam and the tunnel rats."

After they had pulled Flowers out of the hole and had been told there was nobody down there, nothing was said—but they all knew. Flowers's own strict rules would have to be applied to him as ruthlessly as to any other tunnel rat. Sergeant Schultz had gone to the executive officer and told him what had happened: the men's confidence in their leader was shaken; he might be a danger to them. The tunnel rats were sent out on a mission and Flowers was not told about it till they had gone. For the sake of their morale he was quickly shipped out of Lai Khe to Di An, where he was drunk for a week; then to Bien Hoa and home. He had just vanished; there were no farewells, no handovers.

In 1984, in the penthouse restaurant of the Philadelphia skyscraper where he worked as a stock-broker, Jack Flowers ruminated on the end of his war. "Rat Six was dead. He died in some tunnel in the Iron Triangle. Batman had been right. "Charlie didn't get me; I'd gotten myself."

Tunnel life —cave-dwelling, nectar-eating bat *eonycteris spelea*. "You'd be crawling through a really small tunnel, you had just enough room to crawl and you'd kick all these bats up and they'd come flying at you and they'd go right down your back and you could feel them, and they'd get tangled in your hair...you could feel them all the way down your back, over your butt, down your legs, and gone. They used to give me the shivers." —Sgt. Bill Wilson.

War of attrition

From Tet to the Easter Offensive

THE TET OFFENSIVE of January 1968 was the climax of the tunnels' existence. The coordinated series of damaging attacks by the Viet Cong on the capital city, Saigon, was planned and prepared in tunnels in Cu Chi and the Iron Triangle a mere 20 miles away, and at a time when MACV was telling the American public that the war was going its way. Such was the psychological impact of the Tet Offensive that it became the turning point of the war, the beginning of the end. "Without the tunnels," said Lieutenant General Richard Knowles, "you wouldn't have the Tet Offensive." After it, as the decimated guerrillas were increasingly replaced in the fighting by the regular army of North Vietnam, the tunnels' role diminished correspondingly. But in 1968 they were crucial.

The decision to mount the nationwide Tet Offensive was taken at the highest levels of the Lao Dong party in Hanoi. In July 1967 the funeral of General Nguyen Chi Thanh took place in the northern capital. He was the erstwhile military commander of COSVN, who died of cancer. The occasion was the opportunity for a conference of political and military leaders from all over Vietnam. At the urging of General Giap, the chief Communist strategist, they agreed to try to break the stalemate with a general offensive and general uprising at the next lunar new year festival. This would be almost sacrilegious, and would cause deep resentment among ordinary Vietnamese. But its improbability would be its best concealment, as had been the case earlier in history when, in 1789, Vietnamese patriots had used the same trick on the occupying Chinese in Hanoi. The offensive was planned in complete secrecy. The war in South Vietnam was to be taken from the countryside to the

Location of Viet Cong attacks during the Tet Offensive.

139

PLANNING TET:
Mai Chi Tho,
seventh from
right, political
commissar of
the Viet Cong
in the Saigon
area, planning
the Tet
Offensive at a
base at Ben Cat
on the edge of
the Iron
Triangle in
1967. During
the planning
operation, VC
intelligence
officers
infiltrated
Saigon, using
the tunnels as
their base.

towns and cities, where, it was hoped, the people would rally to the National Liberation Front's side and rise up against the South Vietnamese government of President Thieu. This was intended to bring about the collapse of the regime in Saigon and convince the American public in an election year that the war was futile and unwinnable.

The men and the weapons for the attacks in Saigon were assembled in the tunnels of Cu Chi and the Iron Triangle. They were systematically moved up to the edge of the city and, on the eve of the attack, to specially prepared safe houses inside it. The arms were transported in agricultural vehicles, fake funeral processions, and by other devious means. Four thousand guerrillas entered the city with the crowds anticipating the Tet holiday. The Americans were caught off-guard, and subsequent investigation would find a serious intelligence failure.

At the end of January, US and South Vietnamese government installations were attacked at over 100 cities, towns, and bases. Two long sieges—at remote Khe Sanh and the occupied citadel of Hue—prolonged the agony of Tet '68. But the attacks on offices in the heart of Saigon had by far the greatest impact and psychological effect. These self-sacrificial Viet Cong raids turned the war in the Communists' favor. After Tet, many Americans began to doubt if they could achieve anything they might call victory in Vietnam.

The political commissar of the Viet Cong's Military Region IV, Mai Chi Tho, planned the attacks at a tunnel base near Ben Cat in the Iron Triangle. There is a photograph of him taken with a group of earnest young Viet Cong officers, some of them girls, grouped around a table of maps and plans. "During the Tet offensive," he said, "I was in the Iron Triangle. We were working day and night. It was a time of very secret and intensive activity. Many of our officers had to secretly reconnoiter the enemy targets. They moved around in Saigon on forged identity papers. Our fifth columnists, soldiers and officers working inside enemy military installations, came to report. They could come and return to their posts within a few hours. That would not have been possible if the headquarters were too far away; that's why Cu Chi was important. The tunnels were where preparations were made for the offensive, a place for stocking weapons and supplies and assembling troops. They were especially valuable after the offensive failed to achieve its objectives, because they provided a base for preparing subsequent attacks."

All over South Vietnam, towns and cities were hit by the Viet Cong. In Saigon itself, squads of commandos seized the radio station, the Philippine embassy, and other quarters of the city, and assaulted the presidential palace, the headquarters of MACV at Tan Son Nhut air base, and the US embassy, then a newly built defensible structure in concrete on the city's main boulevard. South Vietnamese police fled when the two Viet Cong vehicles drove up in the early hours. A hole was blown in the embassy wall, and the defense was left to US marines and military police on duty. Of the attacking squad, all but one were soon killed, and the raid was dismissed by an American officer on the spot as a "piddling patrol action." But the incident shocked the whole world. Far greater damage was being done elsewhere in Vietnam, where ten provincial capitals fell under temporary Viet Cong control and key American supply bases and airstrips were

Gen. Nguyen Chi Thanh —Viet Cong commander, who died in July 1967. His funeral provided the gathering point at which senior Viet Cong and NVA officials started planning the Tet Offensive.

Gen. Vo
Nguyen Giap
—North
Vietnam's
defense
supremo.
The architect of
the French
defeat at Dien
Bien Phu, he
orchestrated
the war against
American
forces from the
North
Vietnamese
capital of
Hanoi.

bombarded. But the handful of guerrillas who got inside the embassy's wall attracted the attention of the entire Saigon-based press corps, and destroyed years of optimistic public relations efforts by the Joint US Public Affairs Office, the Americans' information operation.

In purely military terms, most of the Viet Cong's Tet operations were failures. But that was irrelevant. It was the moment at which American casualties surpassed those in the Korean War. It was a moment of painful truth—always a rare commodity in Vietnam. The Tet Offensive helped to crystallize public and political opinion on what had always been an "unpopular" war and hence had far-reaching effects.

Ironically, the Tet Offensive was an experience from which the Viet Cong would never recover either. In theory, North Vietnamese infantry battalions were to follow up the initial attacks by the Viet Cong sappers, but the advantage of surprise could not be exploited. Despite the near-perfect coordination of attacks across the country, their impact was dissipated by being so scattered. The attacks were driven off—destructively—everywhere except Hue and Saigon, and the capital was pacified within a week. Over 40,000 Viet Cong guerrillas died in the fighting, crippling the movement beyond repair. There had been no popular uprising in their support; their chances of victory were too uncertain for the pragmatic Vietnamese city-dwellers. Nonetheless, there had been no betrayal of the complex preparations for the offensive. NVA General Tran Van Tra himself conceded that the offensive hurt the attackers as much as the defenders.

But a month after Tet '68, Tran Van Tra ordered further attacks, and yet more throughout 1968, to try to sustain the momentum of the war and dispel the disillusionment on the Communist side engendered by Tet's failure to live up to its idealistic promises. The Viet Cong had to be persuaded that victory was somehow within their grasp, and so the attacks—and the attrition—went on. The American response was a mailed fist. For the remainder of the 1968 dry season, and in the following winter, waves of helicopters and APCs ferried in the troops for huge search-and-destroy operations that swept through Viet Cong base areas. (It was on one such operation that the massacre of villagers at My Lai occurred.)

The depleted guerrillas crept back to their tunnel hideouts, most of their fighting spirit exhausted. "There were only four of us fighters left at Nhuan Duc, next to Cu Chi base," said Captain Nguyen Thanh Linh, their local commander. "We were fighting for a few days in the towns, and left the countryside empty. We poured all our forces out to fight and lost our key cadres. When the Americans counterattacked, we had no good men left. We were nearly out of ammunition. Our food reserve was being used up day by day. Between four men we had just 50 grams of rice a day. We ate fish from the Saigon River and plenty of rats. Some people were worried that Cu Chi might be lost. You could say that the Americans were winning tactically, if not strategically."

Tran Van Tra —NVA military commander in South Vietnam. He later admitted that the Tet Offensive had cost too many Viet Cong lives to be effective.

The Tet attacks on Saigon had originated in the old hornets' nest of Viet Cong in Cu Chi district and the Iron Triangle. This time, the American high command decided to obliterate the tunnel-riddled sanctuaries once and for all by the complete destruction of the ecology. Chemical defoliants had proved only temporarily effective. The Fil Hol plantation, the Ho Bo and Boi Loi woods, and the Iron Triangle were to be systematically flattened by Rome plows. "American grass" was planted from Chinook helicopters and periodically set on fire. This was a specially developed strain of coarse grass that burned easily and quickly. Colonel Thomas A. Ware commanded a battalion of the 25th Infantry on sweep operations. "We spent our time in the Ho Bo woods, and Fil Hol and the Iron Triangle. I think we cut something like 14,000 acres of trees. We'd run into tunnels every day. Sometimes our heavy bulldozers or tanks would collapse them. Sometimes we'd just blow the entrance."

President Lyndon B. Johnson —a political casualty of Tet. Two months after it he announced that he would not run for reelection.

Recalled Mai Chi Tho: "Yes, the Americans bulldozed the whole area; there was not a house or a tree left. One could stand on the bank of the Saigon River and see to Route No. 1 about seven miles away without any obstruction. We had to stay in short sections of tunnel. Our fighting was limited. There were no activities in the daytime, only at night."

The population of villagers had largely vanished already. On average, since 1965, over a million of

South Vietnam's villagers a year had been displaced
or fled the bombs, bullets, and defoliants and had
become refugees in government-controlled cities.
This took away the Viet Cong's tax base, and its life
support. And in a free strike zone, no one would survive for long above ground anyway.

"The trees were stripped of foliage," Captain Linh
recalled. "It was very hot in the tunnels. If we failed
to conceal our footsteps on a path, the helicopters
would have spotted them. The Americans' greatest

War of attrition

CLEARING THE IRON TRIANGLE: A bulldozer proceeds to block a tunnel entrance exposed by land-clearing operations. After the Tet Offensive all the trees in the Iron Triangle were cut down to expose tunnel entrances, creating an inhospitable environment for the Viet Cong.

success at that time was two armed helicopters from the 25th Aviation Battalion—Cobras—on the front of which were painted the pointed teeth and red mouth of a magical beast; we called them the red-headed beasts. They had two gunners—blacks—who were excellent sharpshooters. Just a glimpse of us and they swiveled their gun-pods to shoot and kill instantly; many of our soldiers died. They flew low and fast and were deadly accurate. We made dummies holding rifles up so that we could attract them and shoot at them, and one crashed at Cu Chi base camp. We buried the victims of the red-headed beasts all in the same place as a warning to everyone. There were 50 or 60 graves, one added every two or three days. The cemetery no longer exists now."

This was the darkest hour. Ironically, as the last American units pulled out in the early 1970s, the Viet Cong were admitting defeat. Their hardships were so severe that even the resolute Captain Linh admitted that in 1969 and 1970 morale collapsed and there were many deserters from the Viet Cong, Hoi Chanhs. "There was just too much hardship at that time; the slightest mistake could have been fatal."

In February 1970 he was living with the remnants of his squad in a tunnel a few hundred yards from the perimeter of Cu Chi base camp. It was the same tunnel from which the Dac Cong had emerged for the attack on 26 February 1969 that destroyed so many helicopters on the base. Linh recalled: "Every day American troops passed over my head. They had no idea we were there, so did not look for us. We heard the metal tracks of patrolling tanks screeching all night long. We heard the Americans joking and laughing. We lived there a whole month, but after I left that place I was caught." Captain Linh's war was over; he was a prisoner after five years in the tunnels.

INFLAMMABLE GRASS:
A Viet Cong veteran holds up some "American grass"— a special strain of coarse grass planted from the air that burned easily and quickly when torched with napalm. It was scattered all over the Iron Triangle.

As a result of the growing number of deserters, the Viet Cong suffered yet another setback that hastened their collapse.

Outside the free strike zones the Viet Cong still had a political and community infrastructure in the villages. Using intelligence derived from defectors, the Americans proposed to expose the tunnel hideouts of the cadres and root out the NLF infrastructure completely.

Phoenix, as this program was called, was devised by Robert Komer, a former CIA man and General Westmoreland's deputy for pacification. He was nicknamed Blowtorch, and created in 1967 a scheme called CORDS (Civil Operations and Revolutionary Development Support), which President Thieu's government reluctantly accepted. Phoenix was its key element, to be implemented by South Vietnamese police, troops, and irregulars under CIA direction, in accordance with President Nixon's policy of Vietnamization, applied from 1969 onward. The object of the Phoenix program was to identify and root out

DEATH FROM ABOVE: **AH-1G Cobra helicopters, operating from Cu Chi base, picked off Viet Cong guerrillas when they emerged from their tunnels in the newly defoliated naked landscape of the Iron Triangle.**

PSYOPS: A propaganda team broadcasting messages through a loudspeaker to Viet Cong in nearby tunnels to induce them to defect. As conditions in the tunnels worsened, desertions increased.

the secret Communist apparatus in South Vietnam. In the early 1960s the Viet Cong had crippled the administration of the Saigon government by the systematic murder of appointed village chiefs and other officials. If the NLF's local organization of cadres, activists, and helpers could be wiped out, then it was hoped a recurrent pattern could be broken: the cycle in which guerrilla units, ground down by American military action, were rebuilt time after time by the NLF working among the population. In any event, the Phoenix program produced a tangle of graft, inefficiency, brutality, and murder. But combined with the depopulation of the countryside, it succeeded in gravely damaging the Viet Cong's organization, compromising the tunnels, and forcing General Tran Van Tra to rely instead upon the regular divisions of the North Vietnamese army.

But the most decisive blow against tunnels came from the air. On 31 October 1968, President Johnson had ordered an end to the bombing of North Vietnam as a gesture to hasten the convening of peace talks in Paris. Strategic Boeing B-52s, adapted to carry over 100 "iron" bombs each, had long been flying missions from their bases at Andersen Air Force Base on Guam and U-Tapao, Thailand. These huge, high-flying aircraft never saw their targets; they were guided in and their bombing was directed by ground radar up to 200 miles away. They were not allowed to bomb within a 3-kilometer radius of error next to friendly forces. After the bombing halt in the North, they were more available to ground commanders in South Vietnam. The generals decided to use the bombers to saturate the free strike zones with 750- and 500-pound high-explosive bombs.

The bombs were dropped in sticks that left a mile-long swathe of total devastation. The landscape erupted with a string of explosions. Tons of earth—along with trees, buildings, and human bodies—were hurled into the air. A B-52 strike could be seen, heard, and felt for 20 miles: a thunderous symphony of destruction that shook the face of the earth and left it permanently scarred. In Cu Chi and the Iron Triangle there was, by 1969, little vegetation left and few people; only a handful of guerrillas hung on in conditions of extreme privation in the tunnels. For them, the most destructive of the B-52s' bombs were those fused to explode not in the air or on impact but after they had penetrated several feet into the ground. The explosion from one of these created a local earthquake that collapsed the sturdiest of tunnel walls. The resulting craters, which still deface the landscape, were up to 30 feet deep—huge pits that sliced into the tunnel system, making it unusable and irreparable. "A five-meter hole could be sufficient to destroy a tunnel," said Major Nguyen Quot. "B-52 bombs made holes 12 meters deep." Air holes were blocked by debris. When the tunnel system was blocked in several places, air could no longer circulate and the inmates suffocated. Carpet bombing by B-52s gradually succeeded where the CS gas and demolition charges of the tunnel rats had failed—denying the use of the tunnels to the Viet Cong.

But this military success came too late to affect the outcome of the conflict. The long, indecisive war of attrition, the shock of Tet '68, and the war's deep unpopularity at home had already undone America's resolve in Vietnam.

Viet Cong tunnel fighter —the slouch hat and the check scarf were their adopted uniform. Like his US counterpart he carries a flashlight. His rifle is a captured M-14 automatic with a silencer. The cloth rosette on the right of his chest was the VC equivalent of a medal.

THE CEASE-FIRE agreement signed by Henry
Kissinger and Le Duc Tho in Paris, in January 1973,
enabled the United States honorably to disengage
from the war but left the Communists in complete
control of large parts of South Vietnam. Three hundred thousand North Vietnamese troops were
allowed to remain there. Following the Tet Offen-

sive, the ARVN had receded to defend the cities and a few outposts, abandoning the countryside. The NVA consolidated its military presence. When fighting began again in 1973—as it shortly did—the Communists made progressive territorial gains. There were periodic battles between the strengthened and rearmed NVA and a demoralized ARVN

SURRENDER:
Bamboo air
tubes reveal a
spider hole.
Seconds later a
VC surrenders.

throughout 1974. The North Vietnamese began
their final offensive that December. Moving from the
highlands to the coastal plain, and then down to the
piedmont, the North Vietnamese troops surrounded Saigon with a rapidity that surprised even

War of attrition

CARPET BOMBER: B-52 bombers dropped delayed action bombs that penetrated the ground before exploding. These succeeded where the tunnel rats had failed. The bombs demolished large sections of the tunnel system by creating the equivalent of localized earthquakes that sent shock waves through the tunnel structures.

themselves. In April 1975 they were poised to take the city.

The devastated Iron Triangle still had a role to play. Just before the final assault on Saigon, Generals Van Tien Dung (in overall command) and

TAKING SAIGON:
Provinces marked in gray are those that fell in the Communist advance that began in January 1975. By mid-April the Communists had reached Gia Dinh, in which Cu Chi district lies. From its tunnels their leaders directed the final push to take Saigon.

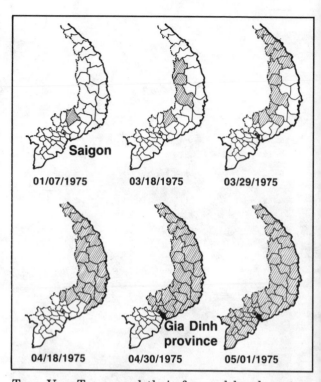

Tran Van Tra moved their forward headquarters from the security of Loc Ninh to what remained of the tunnel base in Ben Cat district, where Mai Chi Tho had planned the Tet Offensive on Saigon in 1967. "It was," said Van Tien Dung in his account of the collapse of South Vietnam, "an old base of one of our special action units from Saigon, northwest of Ben Cat. From this base our special action forces had over the years organized many attacks into Saigon, causing heavy casualties to the Americans and their valets." Two days later two other senior North Vietnamese showed up there, unable to stay away from the action. They were COSVN secretary and politburo member Pham Hung, and Le Duc Tho, politburo member, signatory of the 1973 cease-fire agreement, and Mai Chi Tho's brother. When Vietnam's 30-year war for independence came to its ignominious end, as the tanks converged on Saigon's presidential palace, the generals and politicians who commanded them received the good news, appropriately, at a former tunnel base in the most fought-over cockpit of the long struggle.

War of attrition

VILLAGE VICTORY PARADE:

In 1975 the Viet Cong came out of hiding and the villagers followed the victorious Vietnamese troops into their old villages. The 30 years of fighting—ten of them against American armed forces—were over.

155

ADSID	— Air-delivered seismic intruder-detection device; microphone and transmitter dropped into suspect areas.
AK-47	— Russian-designed Kalashnikov 7.62mm automatic rifle used by Communist troops.
APC	— Armored personnel carrier.
ARVN (Arvin)	— The South Vietnamese army (Army of the Republic of Vietnam).
B-52	— Strategic high-altitude bomber converted for conventional bombing over Vietnam.
Big Red One	— The US 1st Infantry Division.
C-rations	— Combat rations.
Cedar Falls	— Search-and-destroy operation mounted in the Iron Triangle and Cu Chi district in January 1967.
Charlie	— Short for "Victor Charlie," meaning VC or Viet Cong.
Chieu Hoi	— Amnesty program enabling VC to defect with safety to the South Vietnamese government side.
Chinook	— CH-47 cargo helicopter.
Claymore	— Antipersonnel mine that propels shrapnel in a fan-shaped pattern.
Cobra	— AH-1G attack helicopter.
COSVN	— Central Office for South Vietnam: Communist HQ in the South.
Crimp	— Search-and-destroy operation mounted in Cu Chi district in January 1966, followed immediately by Operation Buckskin.
CS	— A riot control gas.
Dac Cong	— Viet Cong special forces.
DEROS	— Date eligible for return from overseas: the end of a GI's tour in Vietnam.
DH-5, DH-10	— Viet Cong claymore (q.v.) mines.
DMZ	— The demilitarized zone between North and South Vietnam.
Dust-off	— Medical evacuation by helicopter.
Fire base	— Remote artillery base.
Frag	— Murder of officers or NCOs by enlisted men; derived from the use of fragmentation grenades.

Glossary

Free strike zone	— Area where everybody was deemed hostile and a legitimate target by US forces.
Gunship	— Armed helicopter.
GVN	— The government of South Vietnam.
Hoi Chanh	— Defector under the Chieu Hoi program.
Iron Triangle	— VC-dominated area between the Thi Tinh and Saigon rivers, next to Cu Chi district.
Kit Carson scouts	— Former Viet Cong acting as guides for US units.
M-16	— US 5.56mm infantry rifle.
M-60	— US 7.62mm machine gun.
MACV (Macvee)	— US Military Assistance Command in Vietnam.
MEDCAP	— Medical civil action program— free treatment for villagers by US and ARVN medics.
Medevac	— Medical evacuation by helicopter.
Mighty mite	— Commercial air blower used for injecting gas into tunnels.
MR IV	— Viet Cong military region surrounding and including Saigon.
NLF	— The National Liberation Front of South Vietnam.
NVA	— The North Vietnamese army.
OJT	— On-the-job training.
Phoenix	— Intelligence-based campaign to eliminate the Viet Cong infrastructure.
PSYOPS	— Psychological operations.
Punji stake	— Sharpened bamboo used in primitive booby trap.
Rome Plow	— Specially designed bulldozer blade for land-clearing.
SP4,SP5	— US Army noncommissioned ranks.
Spider hole	— VC firing position at tunnel opening.
Tet	— Vietnamese lunar new year festival, celebrated as a national holiday.
Tropic Lightning	— The US 25th Infantry Division.

About the authors

**Tom Mangold and
John Penycate**

TOM MANGOLD has been an investigative reporter with BBC-TV's flagship television public affairs show *Panorama* for ten years, during which time he was nominated TV reporter of the year for his investigative work. As a war correspondent he has covered Vietnam, two Middle East wars, Aden, Biafra, and most recently the Russian invasion of Afghanistan. His first book, *The File on the Tsar*, an investigation into the true fate of the last Russian imperial family, became an international best-seller. He currently continues reporting for BBC-TV, and writes at home in West London where he lives with his wife and three daughters. His last remaining hobby is playing the "blues harp"—the harmonica. With John Penycate he coauthored the best-selling *Tunnels of Cu Chi* (Random House, 1985; Berkley, 1986)

JOHN PENYCATE is a correspondent with BBC-TV's *Panorama* public affairs television show. After graduating from Oxford University, he worked at Britain's Independent TV network with David Frost, before joining BBC-TV. Many of his reports have been rebroadcast by CBS's *Sixty Minutes*, or on PBS. He has made documentaries in many countries, including Vietnam, Argentina during the Falklands war, Afghanistan, and Lebanon. He produced the first BBC report from Vietnam after the Communist victory. He visits the USA regularly and has many friends on both coasts. His favorite relaxation is skiing. His first book, *Psychopath*, a study of a mass murderer, appeared in 1976. He lives with his wife in London. With the proceeds of the *Tunnels of Cu Chi* he bought himself the expensive toy that affords him most innocent pleasure—a Porsche.

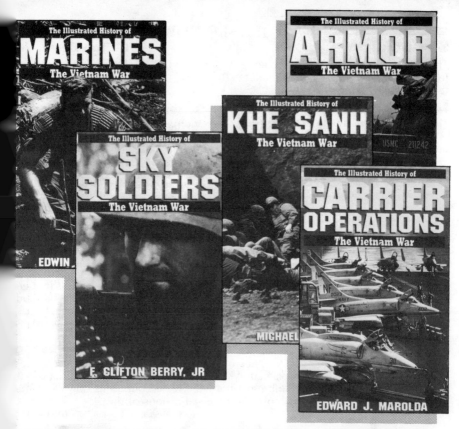

THE ILLUSTRATED HISTORY OF THE VIETNAM WAR

ntam's Illustrated History of the
etnam War is a unique and new
ies of books exploring in depth the
r that seared America to the core:
war that cost 58,022 American lives,
at saw great heroism and re-
urcefulness mixed with terrible
struction and tragedy.

he Illustrated History of the Viet-
m War examines exactly what hap-
ned: every significant aspect—the
ysical details, the operations and
the strategies behind them—is analyz-
ed in short, crisply written original
books by established historians and
journalists.

Some books are devoted to key battles and campaigns, others unfold the
stories of elite groups and fighting
units, while others focus on the role
of specific weapons and tactics.

Each volume is totally original and
is richly illustrated with photographs,
line drawings, and maps.